GARY CLYDE HUFBAUER
KIMBERLY ANN ELLIOTT

Measuring the Costs of Protection in the United States

Institute for International Economics
Washington, DC
January 1994

Gary Clyde Hufbauer is the *Reginald Jones Senior Fellow* at the Institute. He was formerly Marcus Wallenberg Professor of International Finance Diplomacy at Georgetown University (1985–92), Deputy Director of the International Law Institute at Georgetown University (1979–81); Deputy Assistant Secretary for International Trade and Investment Policy of the US Treasury (1977–79); and Director of the International Tax Staff at the Treasury (1974–76). He has written extensively on international trade, investment, and tax issues, including *NAFTA: An Assessment* (rev. 1993), *US Taxation of International Income* (1992), *North American Free Trade* (1992), *Economic Sanctions Reconsidered* (second edition 1990), *Trade Policy for Troubled Industries* (1986), and *Subsidies in International Trade* (1984).

Kimberly Ann Elliott, *Research Associate,* is coauthor of *Economic Sanctions Reconsidered* (second edition 1990), *Auction Quotas and United States Trade Policy* (1987), and *Trade Protection in the United States: 31 Case Studies* (1986).

INSTITUTE FOR INTERNATIONAL ECONOMICS
11 Dupont Circle, NW
Washington, DC 20036-1207
(202) 328-9000   FAX: (202) 328-5432

C. Fred Bergsten, *Director*
Christine F. Lowry, *Director of Publications*

Cover design by Michelle M. Fleitz

Printed in the United States of America
97 96 95 94   5 4 3 2

Library of Congress Cataloging-in-Publication Data

Measuring the costs of protection in the United States
   Gary Clyde Hufbauer and Kimberly Ann Elliott
      p.   cm.
   Includes bibliographical references and index.
   1. Tariff—European Economic Community countries.
   2. Tariff—United States.
   I. Hufbauer, Gary Clyde.
HF2040.5.Z7M43   1993
382.7—dc20   93-5022
                                                   CIP

ISBN 0-88132-108-7

Marketed and Distributed outside the USA and Canada by Longman Group UK Limited, London

The views expressed in this publication are those of the authors. This publication is part of the overall program of the Institute, as endorsed by its Board of Directors, but does not necessarily reflect the views of individual members of the Board or the Advisory Committee.

Contents

Preface

The Institute has maintained an active interest in the impact of trade restrictions on the economies of the United States and other major countries. William Cline and I in *The United States–Japan Economic Problem* (1985, revised 1987), and more recently Marcus Noland and I in *Reconcilable Differences? United States–Japan Economic Conflict* (1993), estimated the effect of Japanese import barriers on American exports. Gary Hufbauer and Jeffrey Schott, in *NAFTA: An Assessment* (1993), estimated the benefits to the US economy of freer trade with Mexico.

We have also devoted considerable attention to the costs and benefits of America's own trade protection. Gary Hufbauer, Diane Berliner, and Kimberly Elliott published the most extensive analysis to date in their *Trade Protection in the United States: 31 Case Studies* (1986). Cline addressed the most protected manufacturing sector in great detail in *The Future of World Trade in Textiles and Apparel* (1987, revised 1990). Elliott, Schott, Wendy Takacs, and I analyzed the effects of "voluntary" export restraints (VERs) in *Auction Quotas and United States Trade Policy* (1987). On the other side of the trade equation, J. David Richardson has recently authored *Sizing Up U.S. Export Disincentives* (1993).

This new volume, however, represents our first effort to provide a comprehensive analysis of American barriers to imports (including VERs). It assesses their costs to American consumers and their benefits to domestic producers (and to the US Treasury, which receives the tariff revenues), and thus their net impact on the economy. It calculates the job effects of the barriers and the consequent cost to consumers and the economy as a whole.

This study also represents the first installment of an effort to compare the impact of trade protection in the United States with similar policies in the other economic superpowers—Japan and the European Union (formerly the European Community). We hope to publish the Japanese analysis in the near future; a summary statement of some of its preliminary results was included in *Reconcilable Differences? United States–Japan Economic Conflict.* The intended European leg of the project has been substantially delayed but we hope to complete it at a later stage.

Trade policy has become an extremely active topic of public debate in the United States, due largely to the controversy over NAFTA and to the subsequent conclusion of the Uruguay Round in the GATT. One important element of this debate is the impact of America's trade restrictions on its own economy. We hope that this study will provide a foundation for future discussion of, and policy toward, import protection in this country.

The Institute for International Economics is a private nonprofit institution for the study and discussion of international economic policy. Its purpose is to analyze important issues in that area, and to develop and communicate practical new approaches for dealing with them. The Institute is completely nonpartisan.

The Institute is funded largely by philanthropic foundations. Major institutional grants are now being received from the German Marshall Fund of the United States, which created the Institute with a generous commitment of funds in 1981, and from the Ford Foundation, the William and Flora Hewlett Foundation, the William M. Keck, Jr. Foundation, the C. V. Starr Foundation, and the United States–Japan Foundation. The Dayton Hudson Foundation provides support for the Institute's program of studies on trade policy. A number of other foundations and private corporations also contribute to the highly diversified financial resources of the Institute. About 16 percent of the Institute's resources in our latest fiscal year were provided by contributors outside the United States, including about 7 percent from Japan.

The Board of Directors bears overall responsibility for the Institute and gives general guidance and approval to its research program—including identification of topics that are likely to become important to international economic policymakers over the medium run (generally, one to three years), and which thus should be addressed by the Institute. The Director, working closely with the staff and outside Advisory Committee, is responsible for the development of particular projects and makes the final decision to publish an individual study.

The Institute hopes that its studies and other activities will contribute to building a stronger foundation for international economic policy around the world. We invite readers of these publications to let us know how they think we can best accomplish this objective.

C. FRED BERGSTEN
Director
December 1993

Acknowledgments

Because of the size and data requirements of this study, we have more than the usual debts to acknowledge. First, we would like to thank C. Fred Bergsten, Richard N. Cooper, Robert Z. Lawrence, J. David Richardson, and David G. Tarr for carefully reading and commenting on the manuscript. We would also like to thank Angela Barnes for typing drafts of the manuscript, Valerie Norville for helping us make the presentation as reader-friendly as possible, and Christine Lowry and Brigitte Coulton for shepherding the book through the publications process.

Indispensable to the process are several research assistants who collected and scrutinized the data, including Alia Ghandour, Magnus Lambsdorff, Jason Lorber, Rosa Moreira, Brett Parker, Lee Remick, and Peter Weinzierl. We are especially grateful, however, to Johanna Buurman and Anup Malani for their many and varied efforts updating and organizing the data, writing case summaries, and drafting parts of the manuscript. Finally, the authors acknowledge the contribution made by Peter P. Uimonen, who vastly simplified our lives by putting the model in a simple worksheet format.

It was a group effort and we thank you all.

1

Trade Protection in the United States

In 1930, the US Congress passed the now-famous Smoot-Hawley tariff legislation. That law raised average US tariffs on dutiable imports to 59 percent by 1933. Partly as a consequence of ensuing foreign retaliation, which further contracted demand for US goods, the United States slid faster and deeper into the Great Depression. Following World War II, the United States and its allies laid the foundation for an enlightened international trade regime with the creation of the General Agreement on Tariffs and Trade (GATT). As a result of multilateral negotiations under the GATT, average US tariffs on dutiable imports declined from 20 percent in 1947 to 5 percent in 1992. Average tariffs in other developed countries declined similarly.

Despite this generally liberalizing trend, a few favored sectors—most notably parts of agriculture, maritime services, and textiles and apparel—have bucked the trend and shielded themselves from import competition for decades (two centuries in the case of maritime). Meanwhile, pressures for increased protection on behalf of other import-competing industries have not disappeared; typically such pressures become most acute when the economy slows or when the dollar becomes overvalued. With three years of negative or slow growth at the beginning of the 1980s and a 30 percent appreciation in the real, trade-weighted value of the dollar from 1981 to 1985, pressures for import relief became intense. "Voluntary" export restraints (VERs) were negotiated with Japan on automobiles and with the European Community, Japan, and a number of other countries on steel. Import quotas were imposed on sugar, and the quantitative restrictions (QRs) on textile and apparel imports were significantly tightened. In 1986, VERs were negotiated with Japan and Taiwan to limit exports of machine tools to the United States.

Also during this period, "unfair" trade laws—primarily the antidumping and countervailing duty (ADD and CVD) statutes—came to replace the "fair" trade statutes (principally the escape clause) as a principal release valve for trade pressures (see Destler 1992). In response to several antidumping petitions filed in 1985, including one initiated by the US Department of Commerce, Japanese semiconductor producers under the supervision of the Ministry of International Trade and Industry (MITI) raised prices and cut production and exports. At the end of 1986, Canada agreed to impose a 15 percent export tax on shipments of softwood lumber to the United States in order to settle a countervailing duty case brought by US industry.

In the late 1980s, however, the dollar depreciated to a significant extent, US exports grew strongly, and the US trade deficit declined sharply. By 1988, exchange rate changes had significantly reduced the protective effect of the VERs then in place on automobiles and steel, and pressures for new protection abated. The respite was brief. At the beginning of the 1990s, the United States, followed by much of the rest of the world, entered a shallow but prolonged recession; as of mid-1993, only sluggish growth had been restored in the United States. Bilateral relations with Japan were also exacerbated by renewed depreciation of the yen in 1989–90, which resulted in record Japanese trade surpluses in 1992–93.

In early 1992, pressure from Congress and the US auto industry forced the Japanese government to lower the ceiling on its VER from 2.3 million vehicles per year—a level not reached in several years due to growing transplant production—to 1.65 million per year, 5 percent below the 1991 actual level of exports. In the summer of 1993, the US International Trade Commission ruled that US steel producers had been injured by dumped and subsidized imports of cold-rolled, plate, and corrosion-resistant steel from a number of countries. Still, the auto VER was probably not binding in 1992 or 1993 because of continuing sluggishness in the US economy and the appreciation of the yen against the dollar in 1991–92, and the antidumping and countervailing duties imposed on some steel products affected only a small portion of total US steel imports.[1]

In addition to having relatively high or unusual protection, the 21 sectors examined in detail in this chapter are those having a domestic market of at least $1 billion and potential imports following liberalization

---

1. Also, during the summer 1993 congressional debate over the budget bill, a little-noticed provision requiring that US-made cigarettes include at least 75 percent American-grown tobacco was inserted (*New York Times*, 29 September 93, 41). No attempt has been made here to quantify the effects of the provision.

of about $100 million or more. These selection criteria, then, exclude some high tariff cases with markets smaller than $1 billion (USITC 1989a).[2] Thirteen of the cases included in this study involve tariffs of close to 10 percent or higher; three concern agricultural products protected by statutory import quotas, while another case involves a statutory ban on foreign shipping between US ports; three other sectors, including textiles and apparel, were protected by VERs. Finally, softwood lumber is included, even though the average price impact of the CVD settlement was only 6.5 percent in 1990 because of the high political profile of that case. Table 1.1 shows that, with the exception of softwood lumber and machine tools, the sectors studied here have been shielded from imports for 35 years or more.

One reason for the persistence of trade barriers in some sectors, and their cyclical recurrence in others, is that the costs of maintaining the barriers are often obscure. This study seeks to bring greater transparency to the costs and benefits of protection. The computable partial equilibrium model used to calculate the welfare and other effects of US trade barriers is spelled out in chapter 2.[3] The three key assumptions in that model are that all markets are perfectly competitive, that the imported good and the domestic good are imperfect substitutes, and that foreign supply is perfectly elastic—in other words, that changes in the level of imports do not affect the world price of the good. Potential effects of these simplifying assumptions as well as qualifications of and extensions to the model are discussed at the end of the chapter.

The Costs and Benefits of US Trade Protection in 1990

The potential consumer gains if the United States eliminated *all* tariffs and quantitative restrictions on imports are in the neighborhood of $70 billion—about 1.3 percent of the US GDP in 1990. This figure reflects

---

2. Among the sectors included in the USITC study but excluded here are leather gloves and mittens, nonstuffed dolls, certain bicycles, and optical instruments.

3. Because various sectors of the economy are interrelated, a general equilibrium model is the preferred method for measuring the aggregate effects of protection across industries. Adding up separately calculated partial equilibrium estimates, as is done below, may result in the aggregate effects being either understated or overstated, depending on the interrelationships among products subject to liberalization. See Tarr and Morkre (1984) for further discussion of these issues. Computable general equilibrium treatments of the welfare effects of US trade barriers may be found in de Melo and Tarr (1992) and USITC (1993). The results of those studies are not presented here because, aside from the differences in partial and general equilibrium modeling, other differences in base year, sectoral coverage, and the measurement of welfare make comparisons among the various estimates difficult.

Table 1.1 Characteristics of 21 protected industries, 1990

Product category[a]	Protection initiated (year)	Domestic shipments (millions of dollars)	Imports, cif, duty paid (millions of dollars)	Production workers (thousands)	Hourly wages for production workers (dollars)	Average annual change, 1986–90[b]	
						In employment (percent)	In imports (percent)
Protected by high tariffs							
Ball bearings	1930	1,386	485	15.0	13.03	3.71	9.54
Benzenoid chemicals	1922	14,763	2,057	13.9	16.84	0.40	6.78
Canned tuna	1951	902[c]	339[d]	11.0[d]	4.77	−3.79	8.02
Ceramic articles	1930	371	819	4.1	9.55	−4.48	4.32
Ceramic tiles	1930	650	575	8.1	9.24	2.48	8.62
Costume jewelry	1930	1,417	621	13.1	6.65	−1.75	1.46
Frozen concentrated orange juice	1930	1,185[c]	809	8.9	8.08	0.53	0.41
Glassware	1922	3,898	949	34.8	11.63	−0.55	3.36
Luggage	1930	1,064	1,202	7.5	6.91	−2.00	9.03
Polyethylene resins	1930	7,686[e]	571	11.9	14.76	4.90	37.70
Rubber footwear	1930	597	843	8.8	6.66	−3.90	17.52
Softwood lumber	1987	8,657[c]	2,916	61.1	10.81	−5.10	−1.11
Women's footwear, except athletic	1930	1,325	3,245	22.8	6.13	−5.90	5.73
Women's handbags	1930	453	1,003	10.6	6.08	−9.20	6.06

Protected by import quotas						
Agriculture						
Dairy products	1953	21,300	520	96.0	10.56[f]	0.19	2.90
Peanuts	1953	1,017[d]	1[d]	23.0	6.80	negl.	negl.
Sugar	1934	2,945	992	12.2	11.73[f]	−2.53	−5.00
Maritime[g]	1789	6,500	1,227	20.0	13.92	n.a.	n.a.
Protected by "voluntary" export restraints						
Apparel	1957	61,692	27,641	871.3	6.57	−1.59	10.48
Textiles	1957	64,986	7,079	594.0	8.01	−0.38	15.96
Machine tools	1987	1,203	1,006	10.9	12.31	−2.09	2.51
Total		203,996	54,901	1,827.6	7.76[h]	−1.14[h]	9.40[h]

cif = costs, insurance, and freight; n.a. = not available.

a. Only sectors with a tariff of 9 percent or above, or other unusual protection, US apparent consumption valued at more than $1 billion, and potential imports (after liberalization) of $100 million are included.

b. Employment data for ball bearings is for 1987–90; for canned tuna, 1986–89; for softwood lumber, 1989–91; and for frozen concentrated orange juice, 1987–91.

c. Production, rather than shipments, data are used.

d. The base year is 1989.

e. Domestic sales data are used.

f. In processing.

g. Jones Act trade only; imports in this case are foreign ships moving on inland US waterways, though not between US ports, which is prohibited by the Jones Act.

h. Weighted average; the simple averages are, in order of the columns, 9.57, −1.48, 6.87.

some $32 billion in consumer surplus losses from the unusually high trade barriers in the 21 sectors listed in table 1.1, plus an estimated $38 billion in consumer losses from the imposition of all other tariffs, which average 3.5 percent on other dutiable imports; about a third of US imports are duty-free.[4] The detailed analysis that follows focuses on the 21 highly protected sectors listed in the tables. But the reader should keep in mind that the welfare effects of these exceptional barriers are somewhat less than half of the total welfare losses from all forms of US protection.

Together, the 21 cases cover a domestic market worth almost $200 billion, or about 5 percent of total private consumption (and 3.6 percent of GNP). Overall, the value of domestic production in these sectors is nearly four times the value of imports. Domestic firms in these sectors employ over 1.8 million production workers—1.5 percent of total US employment in 1990. Imports in the 21 sectors total $55 billion, about 10.6 percent of all US merchandise imports in 1990. Despite the import-dampening effects of the trade barriers in these sectors, the value of imports tends to continue increasing, while employment usually declines on average. As noted previously in *Trade Protection in the United States* (Hufbauer, Berliner, and Elliott 1986, 20),

> Special protection as practiced in the United States cannot, for the most part, be faulted for freezing the status quo. Instead, it should be criticized for providing rather little assistance to workers and firms that depart the troubled industry; for imposing huge costs on consumers; for not promoting a smooth transition to the realities of international competition; and for engendering widespread opposition to trade liberalization.

The estimated gains from liberalization are based on the assumption that high tariffs are reduced to zero and that quantitative restrictions are removed but that normal, low tariffs are left in place in the quota cases. The results for textiles and apparel represent the effects of removing both QRs and the high tariffs protecting those sectors.[5] Table 1.2 details the sectoral results of the welfare calculations. Some readers may be puzzled by the relatively small role given to agriculture in table 1.2 ($2.6 billion in consumer surplus gains for dairy, peanuts, and sugar combined) given the recent publicity by GATT Director Peter Sutherland and others to Organization of Economic Cooperation and Development (OECD) estimates that consumers subsidize farmers by as much $20

---

4. The $38 billion is a crude estimate calculated using the computable partial equilibrium model described in chapter 2. It assumes that the weighted averages of the elasticities of supply and demand used in the 21 case studies approximate the average elasticities in the rest of the economy.

5. Apart from textiles and apparel, the tariffs on the other quota-protected products are all less than 10 percent.

Box 1.1 Comparison with OECD estimates

In August 1993, the GATT Secretariat issued a brief report summarizing the costs of selected trade barriers to consumers around the world. Included in the report was an OECD estimate that total transfers to agricultural producers in the United States in 1992 were more than $90 billion. For 1990, our base year, the OECD estimated that *net* transfers to US agricultural producers totaled $33 billion (GATT 1993; OECD 1993). These figures are not comparable to our estimates, however, because they include direct payments and other forms of support financed with tax dollars. The OECD has also estimated the consumer subsidy equivalent (CSE) portion of these transfers, which purports to measure the *implicit* tax imposed on consumers by border measures and other policies that raise the price of agricultural products. The CSE should be roughly comparable to our estimates of consumer surplus losses, but the OECD estimate for 1990, $18 billion for all agricultural products, is significantly higher than our estimate of $2.6 billion for the consumer costs of protecting dairy, peanuts, and sugar.

The difference in the OECD and our estimates can be traced to two sectors: meat, with a 1990 CSE of $6.0 billion, and dairy products, with a 1990 CSE of almost $11 billion. Meat is excluded from our study because there were no import restrictions in place in 1989–90.[1] And the OECD's CSE estimate for dairy products is far higher than our estimated consumer surplus loss of $1.2 billion, primarily because it includes fluid milk, which is not widely traded in world markets. Cheese, which accounts for more than 90 percent of US imports of dairy products, dominates our estimates for the dairy sector but represents only about 10 percent of the total volume of US dairy consumption.

---

1. The Meat Import Act authorizes the US secretary of agriculture to impose import quotas when meat imports are projected to exceed a statutorily derived target level. Actual imports did not reach the target level in either 1989 or 1990 and slightly exceeded the target level in 1991, even though export restraint agreements were negotiated with New Zealand and Australia, the major suppliers. The US International Trade Commission (1990, 3–25) could find little evidence that quantitative limitations on meat imports significantly affected prices in the US market in the years they analyzed. Meat was included in the predecessor to this volume, where we found a 1983 consumer surplus loss from the meat VERs of $1.8 billion (Hufbauer, Berliner, and Elliott 1986, 323).

billion per year. The OECD estimates, however, are not comparable to the estimates here for a number of reasons, as explained in box 1.1.

Domestic producer surplus losses account for half of the $32 billion in potential consumer gains from liberalization of the 21 specially protected sectors. This $16 billion producer loss, on average, equals almost 8 percent of the 1990 value of shipments of the affected industries. The US government would lose nearly $6 billion in tariff revenues if the sectors were liberalized, about 0.5 percent of total government revenue in 1990. The net national welfare gain from liberalization in these sectors amounts to an estimated $10 billion, with more than two-thirds being quota rents

Table 1.2 Estimated welfare effects of liberalizing 21 protected sectors, 1990 (millions of dollars)

Product category	Tariff or equivalent, as percentage of world price	Induced increase in cif value of imports[a]	Consumer surplus gain (A+B+C+D)[b]	Producer surplus loss (A)	Tariff revenue loss (B)	Quota rent gain[c] (C)	Efficiency gain (D)	Net national welfare gain (C+D)	Producer surplus loss as a percentage of base-year shipments
Protected by high tariffs									
Ball bearings	11.0	12	64	13	50	n.a.	1	1	0.94
Benzenoid chemicals	9.0	223	309	127	172	n.a.	10	10	0.86
Canned tuna	12.5	68	73	31	31	6	4	10	3.44
Ceramic articles	11.0	41	102	18	81	n.a.	2	2	4.85
Ceramic tiles	19.0	25	139	45	92	n.a.	2	2	6.91
Costume jewelry	9.0	122	103	46	51	n.a.	5	5	3.25
Frozen conc. orange juice (avg. 1988–91)	30.0	232	281	101	145	n.a.	35	35	6.63
Glassware	11.0	166	266	162	95	n.a.	9	9	4.16
Luggage	16.5	321	211	16	169	n.a.	26	26	1.52
Polyethylene resins	12.0	339	176	95	60	n.a.	20	20	1.23
Rubber footwear	20.0	116	208	55	141	n.a.	12	12	9.25
Softwood lumber	6.5	363	459	264	183	n.a.	12	12	3.05
Women's footwear, except athletic	10.0	216	376	70	295	n.a.	11	11	5.28
Women's handbags	13.5	195	148	16	119	n.a.	13	13	3.53

Protected by import quotas								
Agriculture								
Dairy products (avg. 1989–91)	50.0	417	1,184	835	n.a.	244	104	104	4.04
Peanuts (avg. 1988–89)	50.0	87	54	32	n.a.	negl.	22	22	3.12
Sugar	66.0	557	1,357	776	n.a.	396	185	581	26.35
Maritime	85.0	1,296	1,832	1,275	n.a.	0	556	556	19.62
Protected by "voluntary" export restraints								
Apparel	48.0	9,660	21,158	9,901	3,545	5,411	2,301	7,712	15.98
Textiles	23.4	1,541	3,274	1,749	632	713	181	894	2.69
Machine tools (avg. 1989–90)	46.6	151	542	157	n.a.	350	35	385	13.14
Total	35.2[d]	16,146	32,316	15,784	5,861	7,120	3,546	10,422	7.74[d]

cif = costs, insurance, freight; n.a. = not applicable.

a. In terms of the notation in chapter 3, this column is calculated as $Pm' (Qm' - Qm)$.

b. May not add due to rounding.

c. In all cases except dairy products, the quota rents are assumed to be captured by foreign exporters prior to liberalization. In the dairy case, quota rents are assumed to be captured by licensed US importers; therefore, this transfer is from US importers to US consumers and is not included in the calculation of the net national welfare gain.

d. Weighted average.

Figure 1.1 Distribution of consumer surplus gain from eliminating all US tariffs and nontariff barriers

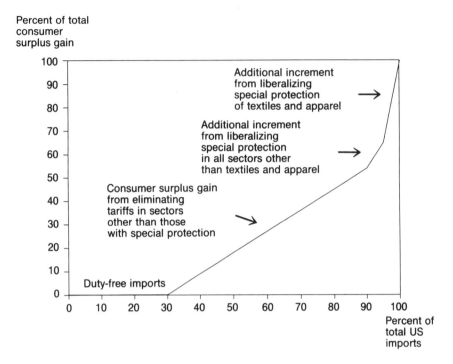

Percent of total consumer surplus gain

Additional increment from liberalizing special protection of textiles and apparel →

Additional increment from liberalizing special protection in all sectors other than textiles and apparel →

Consumer surplus gain from eliminating tariffs in sectors other than those with special protection ↘

Duty-free imports

Percent of total US imports

recaptured from foreign exporters and producers, mostly in the textile and apparel sectors. The net national welfare gain in these cases is far higher than the estimated $300 million net national welfare gain from eliminating the 3.5 percent average tariff on other dutiable imports because, in those sectors, the government collects the price premium on the affected imports in the form of tariff revenues.

The results in table 1.2 highlight an important finding: the textile and apparel sectors not only continue to be the Mount Everest of US trade protection, a position they have occupied for years, but also, by 1990 these two sectors together were the only mountain among the remaining foothills. Textiles and apparel alone accounted for three-quarters of the estimated consumer gain from liberalizing special protection in 1990, $24 billion out the $32 billion total. Figure 1.1 illustrates the peak in protection from textiles and apparel. It shows that liberalization on the approximately 60 percent of US imports with an average 3.5 percent ad valorem tariff delivers just over 50 percent of the total potential consumer surplus gain ($38 billion out of $70 billion). Textiles and apparel imports are only about 6 percent of total US imports, but liberalizing trade barriers in these two sectors would account for more than 30 percent of the potential consumer surplus gain ($24 billion).

The employment effects of liberalization are summarized in table 1.3. Direct job losses represent a decrease in the employment opportunities of production workers in the import-competing industry (job losses in related upstream industries are discussed below). Elimination of special protection in these sectors might reduce employment in these sectors by 192,000 production workers, which represents about 10 percent of the total production work force in the protected industries. Assuming no offsetting policies or employment gains in downstream sectors, these layoffs would increase the national unemployment rate by about 0.15 percent.

Again, the textile and apparel industries dominate, with nearly 90 percent of the estimated job losses occurring in those sectors alone. Cline (1990, 262–64), however, has estimated that gradual liberalization of the textile and apparel sectors—elimination of the VERs and reduction in tariffs to 10 percent and 15 percent for textiles and apparel, respectively, over a period of 15 to 20 years—might not displace workers in those industries faster than would otherwise occur from people retiring or quitting, assuming no new entry.

The cost to the economy and to consumers of preserving these jobs is quite high. In a fourth of the 21 sectors shown in table 1.3, the consumer cost per job saved is $500,000 or more. There is only one sector (costume jewelry) in which the estimated cost of saving a job through trade protection is less than $100,000. On average, the consumer surplus loss per job saved is an astounding $170,000 per year. In other words, consumers pay over six times the average annual compensation of manufacturing workers to preserve jobs through import restraints. But in two-thirds of the cases listed in table 1.1, production workers' hourly wages (excluding compensation) are at or *below* the average hourly manufacturing wage in 1990 of $10.80.[6] In terms of net national welfare, the cost per protected job is about $54,000. This figure far exceeds the cost per worker of even a "gold-plated" adjustment program entailing income maintenance, retraining, and relocation.[7]

---

6. Using detailed data on wage differentials across industries, *after* adjustment for skill differences, Katz and Summers (1989, 264) found that workers in import-intensive industries earned an average of 15 percent less than the average manufacturing worker in 1984. Of the nine sectors they identify as the most import-intensive, seven have negative wage differentials ranging from 10 percent for toys to 23 percent for apparel, despite the fact that all seven are protected by above-average tariffs. The two sectors with above-average wage differentials are office and accounting machines (6.8 percent) and motor vehicles (15.5 percent) (Katz and Summers 1989, table 13).

7. Hufbauer and Rosen (1986), the companion volume to Hufbauer, Berliner, and Elliott (1986), presents one version of an adjustment program that would be more generous to affected workers than current programs yet would still cost US taxpayers and consumers far less than the current system of special protection.

Table 1.3 Estimated direct employment effects of liberalization, 1990

Product category	Decrease in domestic production (millions of dollars)[a]	Decrease in employment opportunities (number of workers)[b]	Consumer gain per job lost (dollars)	Net national gain per job lost (dollars)
Protected by high tariffs				
Ball bearings	13	146	438,356	6,849
Benzenoid chemicals	230	216	>1,000,000	46,296
Canned tuna	33	390	187,179	25,641
Ceramic articles	38	418	244,019	4,785
Ceramic tiles	28	347	400,576	5,764
Costume jewelry	115	1,067	96,532	4,686
Frozen concentrated orange juice	101	609	461,412	57,471
Glassware	165	1,477	180,095	6,093
Luggage	25	226	933,628	115,044
Polyethylene resins	192	298	590,604	67,114
Rubber footwear	116	1,701	122,281	7,055
Softwood lumber	86	605	758,678	19,835
Women's footwear, except athletic	218	3,702	101,567	2,971
Women's handbags	32	773	191,462	16,818

Protected by import quotas				
Agriculture				
Dairy products	513	2,378[c]	497,897	43,734
Peanuts	18	397	136,020	55,416
Sugar	548	2,261[c]	600,177	256,966
Maritime	1,434	4,411	415,325	126,049
Protected by "voluntary" export restraints				
Apparel	10,851	152,583	138,666	50,543
Textiles	1,773	16,203	202,061	55,175
Machine tools	169	1,556	348,329	247,429
Total	16,697	191,764	168,520[d]	54,348[d]

a. This column represents the volume effect of liberalization calculated using base-year prices. In terms of the notation in chapter 3, this column is calculated as $Pd(Qd' - Qd)$.

b. The number of direct jobs affected is assumed to be proportional to the volume change in domestic production. For example, for ball bearings the volume of domestic production is expected to decrease from 416 million units to 412 million units. Employment in this industry is thus projected to decrease by $[1-(412/416)]*100 = 0.96$ percent, or from 15,000 to 14,854 production workers.

c. Workers in processing plants only.

d. Weighted average.

Changes in the Profile of US Protection since 1984

The precursor to the present study is *Trade Protection in the United States: 31 Cases* by Hufbauer, Berliner, and Elliott (1986). All the cases of special protection in effect in 1990, except for machine tools and softwood lumber, were also in effect in 1984–85. In addition, in 1984, there were binding VERs on meat, automobiles, and carbon and specialty steel, restrictions on book manufacturing, and escape-clause tariffs on heavy-weight motorcycles. For purposes of comparison, table 1.4 presents the 1990 results along with revised estimates of the costs of protection in 1984, using the data from Hufbauer et al. (1986) and the more systematic methodology and revised elasticity estimates of the present study.

Readers familiar with the 1986 volume will note that the revised 1984 estimates in table 1.4 are much lower than the estimated aggregate welfare effects contained in table 1.4 of the earlier book. This happens despite the fact that we included in the revised 1984 estimates six high tariff cases that we either did not know about in 1984 or that were classified differently at that time (ball bearings, costume jewelry, luggage, polyethylene resins, women's footwear, and women's handbags). The primary reason for the larger welfare effects presented in Hufbauer, Berliner, and Elliott (1986) is that the methodology then used for calculating the cross-price elasticities of demand in some cases produced estimates that were much too high. In addition, because the new methodology uses a computable equilibrium model that solves for postliberalization prices and quantities simultaneously, it ensures that the changes are consistent with one another.

Returning to the more interesting comparison, table 1.4 and figure 1.2 illustrate the rather large decline in the costs of protection between 1984 and 1990 for sectors other than textiles and apparel. But when the rather large increases in the estimated costs from protecting textiles and apparel are taken into account, the aggregate costs of special protection are about the same in 1990 as in 1984 in nominal terms. As a percentage of US GNP, however, the costs to consumers dropped from 0.8 percent in 1984 to about 0.6 percent in 1990. To put it another way, if the consumer costs of special protection had maintained the same share of GNP in 1990 as in 1984, they would have totaled $44 billion rather than $32 billion. The share of total US imports affected by trade barriers dropped from 21.5 percent of all imports in 1984 to only 10.4 percent in 1990.

Excluding textiles and apparel, the consumer surplus loss dropped by more than half, from $15 billion in 1984 to $6 billion in 1990. Still leaving textiles and apparel to one side, the effective end of the restrictive impact of the next two largest QR cases, steel and autos, decreased the value of quota rents transferred to foreign exporters by 80 percent. This in turn lowered the net national welfare loss from the trade barriers remaining in

Table 1.4 Welfare effects of US special protection,[a] 1984 and 1990 (millions of dollars unless noted)

	Textiles and apparel		All other sectors		Total[b]	
	1984	1990	1984	1990	1984	1990
Consumer surplus loss	15,096	24,432	15,358	6,052	30,454	30,484
Percentage of GNP					0.81	0.55
Producer surplus gain	9,336	11,650	6,888	2,859	16,224	14,509
Tariff revenue gain	2,535	4,177	2,883	1,684	5,418	5,861
Quota rent loss	2,291	6,124	4,011	996	6,302	7,120
Efficiency loss	933	2,482	1,974	508	2,907	2,990
Net national welfare loss[c]	3,224	8,606	5,758	1,260	8,982	9,866
Imports in protected sectors	16,498	34,720	56,913	18,954	73,411	53,674
Percentage of all imports	4.8	6.7	16.7	3.7	21.5	10.4
Induced change in:						
Imports (cif valued)	−5,234	−11,201	−14,935	−3,649	−20,169	−14,850
Percentage of all imports	1.5	2.2	4.4	0.7	5.9	2.9
US production	9,993	12,624	5,217	2,639	15,210	15,263
US employment opportunities (number of production workers)	200,521	168,786	46,302	18,567	246,823	187,353
Consumer loss per job gained[d] (dollars)	75,284	144,751	331,692	325,955	123,384	162,709

cif = costs, insurance, freight

a. Because of the difficulty in obtaining consistent, comparable data, these estimates exclude maritime. Thus the results for 1990 differ from those reported in tables 2 and 3.

b. The two sets of estimates have 18 sectors in common. The 1984 estimates also include restrictions on book manufacturing, steel, specialty steel, motorcycles, autos, and meat, which either expired or were no longer binding constraints on imports by 1990. The 1990 estimates include restrictions on imports of softwood lumber and machine tools, which were imposed after 1984.

c. This figure is the sum of quota rents transferred from foreigners and the efficiency gain. In all cases except dairy we assume that foreigners capture the quota rents.

d. Weighted average.

Figure 1.2   Special protection, 1984 and 1990

Billions of dollars

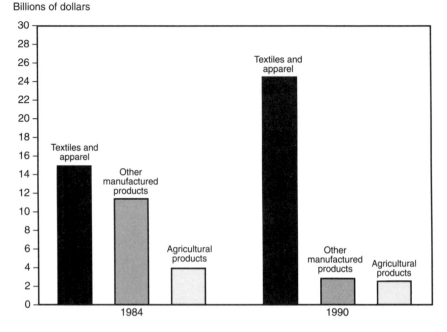

1990 to less than one-fourth what it was in 1984 ($1.3 billion versus $6.0 billion). The steel and auto VERs were still nominally in place in our base year of 1990, but both VERs were negotiated when the dollar was overvalued. Between 1984 and 1990, the dollar's real effective exchange rate dropped from an index value of 100 to just 63, which had the effect of raising the dollar price of US imports substantially. As a result of dollar depreciation and cost-cutting and quality improvements by domestic firms, the levels of steel and auto imports in 1988–89 were below the respective VER ceilings (USITC 1989a and 1989b). In 1989, the VERs on steel were extended for two-and-a-half years at a slightly higher market share, although they were not binding for most categories, and they were allowed to expire in March 1992. Also in 1992, the Japanese government lowered the ceiling for the auto VER, but the lower ceiling still does not appear to have been binding, owing to sluggish growth in the United States. More recent pressures for protection in these two sectors are discussed below.

Thus, in the second half of the 1980s, the depreciation of the dollar, improvements in the trade balance, and relatively strong growth in the United States greatly eased the demands on policymakers to protect vulnerable industries. The new cases that appear on the list for 1990, softwood lumber and machine tools, were both initiated in 1986, when the trade deficit was still growing, though in both cases protection was renewed on more liberal terms in 1991. The semiconductor case, which appears in appendix II but not in the summary tables, was also initiated in 1985–86.[8]

Textiles and apparel are the two big sectors that successfully resisted the trend toward lower trade barriers (figure 2.2). In 1984, liberalization would have improved consumer welfare by $15.1 billion; by 1990, the comparable figure had reached $24.4 billion. By far the largest component of the increase is accounted for by quota rents captured by foreign textile and apparel producers, which more than doubled, from $2.3 billion in 1984 to $6.1 billion in 1990. But even the textile and apparel story is not entirely inconsistent with the liberalization story told above for other sectors.

Most of the tightening of restrictions in these sectors occurred in 1985 and 1986 when the United States negotiated new agreements with major suppliers—Korea, Taiwan, and Hong Kong—that sharply limited growth in imports from those sources (a more restrictive agreement had been negotiated with China in 1983). The United States also insisted on significant tightening of the Multi-Fiber Arrangement when it was renewed in 1986. Although Congress twice passed legislation that would have significantly increased protection of the textile, apparel, and footwear sectors, it was not able in either case to override the presidential veto (Cline 1990). Still, by 1990, the textile and apparel sectors together accounted for 75 percent of the estimated consumer gains from liberalization and nearly 90 percent of the net national welfare gains.

Deflecting Trade Pressures: From Fair to Unfair Trade Relief

Another striking difference between the cases documented in the 1986 study and those studied here is the virtual disappearance of the escape clause as an avenue for import relief. Section 201 of the Trade Act of 1974, known as the escape clause, allows industries to receive import

---

8. Estimates of the effects of the price floor agreement negotiated to settle the antidumping cases brought against Japanese producers of semiconductors are included in the appendix because of the extensive interest in that case. They are not included in the summary tables because we concluded that the price effects of the cartel behavior stimulated by the agreement had been largely dissipated by late 1989 or early 1990. Thus, not only had the protective effects of the semiconductor agreement largely disappeared by 1990 (our base year) but the effects were so transitory—lasting only for six to eight quarters, depending on the product—that they are not comparable to the effects of the other ongoing cases of protection. There is no attempt here to study the potential welfare gains to the United States from the market access part of the agreement, aimed at reducing alleged Japanese barriers to imports of semiconductors.

relief, with no allegation of unfairness, if the industry can persuade the US International Trade Commission that it has suffered "serious injury" and that imports were a "substantial cause," and if the president agrees with the relief recommended by the USITC. In 12 of the 31 cases documented in Hufbauer, Berliner, and Elliott, the escape clause was the avenue of relief for the domestic industry. Since then, only one industry—cedar shakes and shingles—has successfully pursued an escape clause case.[9]

Instead, the "unfair" trade laws have become an increasingly popular path to special protection. This is likely due to the fact that the standard for injury is lower than for the escape clause, and relief is more certain because there is no presidential discretion as to the action to be taken. If "material injury"—injury from imports that is not "inconsequential" or "unimportant"—as a result of "less than fair value" sales is affirmed, antidumping duties are automatically imposed (or other comparable action taken—for example, an agreement by the foreign exporter to restrict sales in the US market). By contrast, in escape clause cases, a US International Trade Commission recommendation for import relief may be overturned by the president. Although the first US antidumping statute was enacted in 1916, the use of antidumping orders to provide extensive protection for the US industry is a comparatively recent phenomenon.

Beginning in 1974, Congress enacted a series of legislative changes that made ADDs a more accessible vehicle of protection. Technical changes in the methods for calculating dumping margins and determining whether injury had occurred contributed to a sharp increase in the number of antidumping petitions in the 1980s.[10] For purposes of this study, we collected data on 119 of the 192 nonsteel antidumping orders in effect at the end of 1991. Individually, many of the antidumping cases affect a rather small market, but collectively, the outstanding antidumping cases for which we have data cover almost $3.2 billion in imports. Weighted by total imports of merchandise in categories subject to an antidumping order ($4.8 billion), the average ADD rate works out to 31 percent.

The set of outstanding antidumping cases can be roughly compared to the special protection afforded in the 21 cases in this study, for which the weighted average duty is 35 percent. Assuming that in aggregate the 21 special protection cases roughly match the product characteristics

---

9. The cedar shakes and shingles case is not included in this study because total US consumption was well under our threshold level of $1 billion (see USITC Pub. 2222).

10. Unlike ADD cases, CVD cases declined after 1985. Of the 392 CVD cases initiated between 1979 and 1990, only 33 were begun after 1987. This decline reflects the emergence between 1982 and 1985 of steel VERs, which were used to settle a number of subsidy complaints. With the expiration of VERs on imported steel in March 1992, however, the number of CVD cases is again beginning to grow.

of the 119 antidumping orders, the economic consequences of eliminating all 119 outstanding ADD orders can be calculated by applying the ratio of the value of US imports subject to antidumping duties (excluding steel) to the value of all US imports covered by special protection—the ratio is 8.1 percent—to the aggregate figures in the summary tables. This calculation suggests that the elimination of the ADD orders would result in an increase in US imports of $1.3 billion, while US consumers would gain $2.6 billion and US producers would lose $1.3 billion. The net national welfare gain of eliminating the ADD orders would amount to about $0.8 billion.

The precise effect of eliminating all ADDs would depend on supply and demand elasticities in each of the sectors protected by antidumping orders, but the foregoing calculations provide a rough and ready insight into the possible impact of ADDs in terms of consumer costs and national welfare. In fact, it is quite possible that this estimate understates the impact of the antidumping statute on US imports and consumer welfare. Though it is difficult to quantify, many observers believe that the costs of responding to an investigation, or just the threat of an unfair trade petition, may cause exporters to either preemptively restrain the quantity of goods they ship to the United States or to maintain prices at a higher level than they otherwise would, even if no duties are ever imposed (Finger 1993, 248). In addition, unfair trade petitions may be used to bring pressure to bear on the government to negotiate a political resolution, as happened in the mid-1980s in the steel and semiconductor cases.

Increasing Pressure: Steel and Autos

A US economic recession in 1990–91 and sluggish global growth since have revived pressures in a protective direction. In 1992, both the steel and auto industries launched new campaigns for relief from import competition. Using the same methodology as in the other cases, we examined the potential impact of new steel and auto trade barriers on US consumers, domestic firms, and American workers. The results are summarized in table 1.5 and explained in more detail in the appendix II case studies.

In March 1992, following expiration of the VERs on steel, several large integrated steel producers brought ADD and CVD cases involving a range of flat-rolled steel products against a large number of foreign suppliers. In June 1993, the Commerce Department made final determinations of dumping margins ranging from 3.65 percent to 109.2 percent (depending on the product and the supplier) and subsidy margins as high as 72.9 percent. In late July 1993, the USITC determined that imports of all hot-rolled and most cold-rolled steel did not cause material injury,

Table 1.5 Estimated welfare effects in other special cases (millions of dollars unless noted)

	Semiconductor agreement (1989)	Steel CVDs and ADDs (1993)	Potentially binding VRA on autos	Potential tariff reclassification for minivans and SUVs
Consumer surplus loss	1,231	1,035	1,741	987
Producer surplus gain	257	657	461	222
Tariff revenue gain	n.a.	318	n.a.	655
Quota rent loss	835	n.a.	1,244	n.a.
Efficiency loss	139	59	36	110
Net national welfare loss	974	59	1,280	110
Induced change in:				
Imports	−1,113	−539	−1,778	−973
US production	536	1,076	507	230
US employment opportunities in the protected industry (number of production workers)	2,342	1,239	1,234	203
Consumer loss per job gained (dollars)	525,619	835,351	>1,000,000	>1,000,000

CVD = countervailing duty; ADD = antidumping duty; VRA = voluntary restraint agreement; SUV = sports utility vehicle; n.a. = not applicable.

Source: Appendix II.

but that most cut-to-length plate and corrosion-resistant steel did cause injury. The final determinations involved producers in 16 countries.

The average of the final ADD and CVD duty margins, for which injury was affirmed, weighted by all imports in the flat-rolled categories, is 13.8 percent. An average increase in the price of flat-rolled steel imports of this amount might induce an estimated 4 percent average increase in domestic prices and could reduce the volume of imports by nearly 30 percent from 6.8 to 5.0 million short tons. As a result, US steel consumers would lose about $1 billion, and US steel producers would gain nearly $700 million. US firms would employ an additional 1,239 steel workers, but each production job created would cost consumers about $84,000. The US Treasury would collect an additional $318 million in duties, while the economy would incur an efficiency loss of $59 million (equal to the net national welfare loss).

Turning to autos, early in 1992, the Japanese government announced that it would lower the export ceiling under its "voluntary" restraint agreement (VRA) to 1.65 million vehicles. The reduction in the ceiling is treated as a hypothetical increase in protection because it was not initially binding owing to sluggish US growth and may not become binding at an exchange rate of 100–110 yen to the dollar, at least as long as no restrictions are placed on transplant production (such restrictions have been considered in proposals debated by Congress in 1992–93). Meanwhile, the US Treasury Department debated the technical merits of reclassifying minivans and sport utility vehicles (SUVs) as light trucks; the US Congress also had under consideration a proposal that would require the US Customs Service to implement the reclassification. A statutory or administrative decision to reclassify would raise the US tariff on minivans and SUVs from 2.5 percent to 25 percent ad valorem.[11]

We looked at the welfare implications of each of these trade measures. First, we modeled the effect of a VRA that reduces Japanese auto exports to the United States from their 1991 levels to 1.65 million units. Assuming that Japanese transplant production would not offset the decline in Japanese auto exports and that European producers would respond by raising prices rather than increasing their market share, consumers could have lost $1.7 billion from the reduction in the VRA level in 1992 if it had been binding. The Big Three's foreign competitors would have gained

---

11. Light trucks imported into the United States pay very high duties because of a trade conflict between the United States and European Community in the 1960s (the so-called "chicken war"). In May 1993, the US Court of International Trade, in *Marubeni America Corp. v. United States*, held that the Nissan Pathfinder, a two-door SUV, should not be reclassified as a cargo vehicle. In October Customs Commissioner George Weise revealed that the administration had suspended its investigation of the reclassification issue pending the outcome of the appeal of the court case (*International Trade Reporter*, 27 October 1993, 1802).

about $1.2 billion in quota rents, while US producers would have gained only about $460 million through increased sales and higher prices. About 1,200 production jobs would have been created in the auto industry. Increasing the tariff on minivans and sport utility vehicles from 2.5 percent to 25 percent ad valorem would also be costly to US consumers (nearly $1 billion in consumer surplus losses), while the US Treasury would be the primary beneficiary, collecting an additional $650 million in tariff revenues. US producers would gain about $220 million.

Qualifications to the Model

Perhaps the biggest obstacle one faces in a venture such as this is the estimation or calculation of the elasticities and other parameters needed to derive the postliberalization equilibrium prices and quantities for the domestic and imported goods. The conversion to the Harmonized Tariff System (HTS) in 1989 and budget cuts affecting technical specialists at the US Bureau of the Census who collect and disseminate economic data also made the construction of a basic data set more difficult than it had been previously.

In addition, the model relies on simplifying assumptions, the effects of which are not easily quantified. First, the base-case model assumes that domestic and import markets are perfectly competitive. In reality, markets may be oligopolistic or otherwise imperfectly competitive. Based on the work of Richardson (1989) and de Melo and Tarr (1992, chapter 7), it seems likely that the assumption of perfect competition causes us to underestimate the costs to consumers of trade protection and the welfare gains that would accrue from liberalization.

Second, in order to simplify calculations and to make the empirical work tractable, we consider only the static, partial equilibrium welfare effects of liberalization. In other words, we consider only the effects *within* a given sector, and we assume no changes in the structure of domestic supply. This analytical method misses the dynamic benefits that may arise from greater competition between imports and domestic products within the sector after liberalization. It also ignores the economywide, or general equilibrium, effects of liberalization in one sector on other sectors in the economy. To be specific, we do not try to calculate the size of any induced downward shift in the domestic supply schedule as a result of greater import competition. Greater technical efficiency (also known as X-efficiency) in the domestic industry could significantly diminish the magnitude of losses incurred by domestic firms and increase the amount of national welfare gains resulting from trade liberalization. Nor do we attempt to estimate the efficiency gains (or losses) that result from changes in other industries once price and exchange rate adjustments have worked through the economy—for example, the benefits of lower input prices for some downstream industries or increased demand for the products of others.

Given these simplifying assumptions, the main ground for argument on our empirical work is the estimation of supply and demand elasticities. Elasticities of supply and demand, and cross-elasticities of demand in import and domestic markets, are the foundation of our model. They determine the size of any domestic market response and the extent of shifts in import and domestic demand curves in response to price changes. Hence, these elasticities play a crucial role in estimating the impact of liberalization. Unfortunately, elasticities of supply and demand are not always available. More serious still, cross-elasticities of demand, which are critical to our two-step model of liberalization, are often not available at all in the literature on individual cases; moreover, when they are available, they are often not reliable. The basic relationships used in calculating the missing elasticities from the parameters available in the literature are described in chapter 2.

A second empirical problem concerns the meshing of systems of categorizing commodities. Data on imports, domestic shipments, and employment often contain frustrating discrepancies that emerge as a consequence of trying to find a concordance between data organized by TSUSA code, HTS code, and SIC code.[12] Up through 1988, the United States classified merchandise imports according to the TSUSA code. In 1989, the United States changed to the HTS; in this process certain TSUSA classifications were truncated or enlarged while others were divided and merged with other classifications to form new HTS classifications. As a result, it is often difficult to construct accurate time-series data on imports.

In certain tariff cases (frozen concentrated orange juice, ball bearings, canned tuna, and polyethylene resins) import figures are reported by HTS code while domestic production and employment figures are reported by SIC code. Unfortunately, many HTS codes overlap two SIC codes, and certain SIC codes include HTS codes that both are and are not subject to high tariff rates. The result is that import figures for certain commodity groups do not correspond exactly to domestic production or employment figures for that commodity. Since the SIC category typically covers a wider range of economic activity than the corresponding HTS category, domestic production and employment figures often had to be adjusted in these cases.[13]

---

12. TSUSA stands for Tariff Schedule of the United States, HTS for the Harmonized Tariff System, and SIC for the Standard Industrial Classification system. The TSUSA and HTS classify products, whereas the SIC system classifies establishments according to lines of production. A given production establishment may turn out more than one product.

13. The maritime case posed special challenges. Since the Jones Act completely bans foreigners from participating in domestic shipping, no directly comparable data on "com-

Extensions of the Model

A partial equilibrium methodology was used because it is simpler and the data requirements far more modest than for general equilibrium modeling. Simplicity and transparency, however, are traded off against complexity and completeness that may more accurately reflect the real world. We have tried to compensate for some of the limitations of the partial equilibrium methodology with supplementary calculations on the impact of liberalization on workers in upstream sectors related to the protected sectors and on terms-of-trade effects.

The first compensating adjustment we made was to calculate a rough and probably high estimate of the potential job losses in related sectors resulting from liberalization of the protected sectors. Ancillary job losses represent possible layoffs by upstream firms that provide inputs used by producers in the 21 industries, plus possible layoffs among nonproduction employees in the protected industries. According to our calculations, which are explained in the notes to table 1.6, liberalization might cause a maximum 130,000 ancillary workers to lose their jobs. As noted in table 1.6, this estimate overstates the employment impact in upstream industries because it does not take into account nonwage value added in those industries. Moreover, this estimate ignores possible ancillary employment gains in "downstream" firms, including export firms, that would be able to purchase cheaper inputs following trade liberalization. Nor does it reflect the likelihood that American households will buy additional quantities of other US products when their budgets are no longer stretched by high-priced imported goods and their also high-priced domestic counterparts.

Combining figures for direct and ancillary jobs losses, we conservatively estimate that, as an upper limit, around 320,000 workers could lose their jobs from trade liberalization in these sectors. To repeat, this figure does not reflect possible job gains in "downstream" industries, including export industries, nor in other sectors of the economy where consumers might direct their extra dollars. In relative terms, the pessimistic figure of 320,000 jobs lost represents less than 0.3 percent of the employed US labor force in 1990. Even the boldest scenario of complete liberalization would require at least five years to dismantle existing trade barriers. Hence, as an outside pessimistic estimate, trade liberalization might dislocate 70,000 production workers per year.[14] By contrast, during 1984–1989, nearly 1.8 million US workers were dislocated annually, for a variety of reasons (Podgursky 1992, 19, table 1).

---

peting" imports are available. Because of this and other problems in making the calculations in this case, it should be treated with special caution (see appendix I).

14. As J. David Richardson points out, the actual figure could be less if anticipated phasing in of liberalization prompts some workers to leave the industry voluntarily.

The second supplementary calculation adjusts for the possibility that the United States is a large enough market to affect world prices. To the extent that US trade barriers drive down world prices of the protected goods, the gains from unilateral import liberalization may be offset to some extent by terms-of-trade losses.[15] Therefore, we modified the computable equilibrium model, relaxing the assumption of perfectly elastic supply, and recalculated the effects of liberalization (see chapter 2). In this exercise, we conservatively assume that world supply elasticities for exports to the United States generally have a value of only 3.0. This low value almost certainly overstates the potential terms-of-trade losses for the United States in most, if not all, sectors. For example, in their general equilibrium analysis, de Melo and Tarr (1992, 103) introduce a terms-of-trade effect only for the automobile sector and use an elasticity of foreign supply of 5.0, higher than the value of 3.0 assumed here.

The results of this exercise are summarized in table 1.7. In the aggregate, the world price of imports in the protected sectors would rise by a weighted average of 9 percent following liberalization. World prices of some imports would rise significantly: peanuts (28 percent), sugar (14 percent), apparel (13 percent), and dairy products (13 percent). Even with the increase in world prices, the prices that US consumers pay for imports in these sectors would decline by more than 30 percent on average after import restraints are lifted. The import prices paid by consumers for apparel (48 percent), machine tools (47 percent), and sugar (43 percent) would decline the most.

If world supply shows as little elasticity across the board as we have assumed, the terms-of-trade losses in the sectors protected by tariffs, plus the dairy quota case, would exceed the net national welfare gains in these same sectors. (though American consumers would still gain substantially from liberalization). The increase in world prices after trade liberalization in these sectors leads to an estimated terms-of-trade loss of $540 million and an overall net national welfare gain from liberalization in all 20 sectors (maritime is excluded) of $8.9 billion, only slightly lower than the $10.3 billion in the base case.

Estimates for the sugar, textiles, apparel, and machine tools cases are not included in this aggregate potential terms-of-trade loss because the theoretical terms-of-trade changes in these four cases are offset by the transfer of the quota rents to foreign producers or foreign exporting firms. In other words, because of the way these quota systems are administered, it is assumed that foreigners (producers or exporters) capture

---

15. In the aggregate, a country's terms of trade may be defined as the weighted average price of its exports divided by the weighted average price of its imports. A reduction in this ratio may be considered a terms-of-trade loss.

Table 1.6 Estimated effect of liberalization on ancillary employment, 1990

Product category	A Decrease in value of domestic production (millions of dollars)[a]	B Nonwage value added (millions of dollars)[b]	C Decrease in direct employment opportunities (number of workers)	D Average earnings per year (dollars)[c]	Residual decrease in domestic production [A − B − (C × D)] (millions of dollars)	Maximum decrease in employment in supplier industries (number of workers)[d]
Protected by high tariffs						
Ball bearings	13	8	146	26,854	1	50
Benzenoid chemicals	230	138	216	36,719	84	2,975
Canned tuna	33	20	390	18,512	6	208
Ceramic articles	38	23	418	13,842	9	333
Ceramic tiles	28	17	347	20,212	4	150
Costume jewelry	115	69	1,067	19,148	26	905
Frozen concentrated orange juice	101	61	609	16,638	30	1,335
Glassware	165	99	1,477	24,977	29	1,030
Luggage	25	15	226	14,265	7	233
Polyethylene resins	192	115	298	33,817	67	2,361
Rubber footwear	116	70	1,701	14,476	22	775
Softwood lumber	86	52	605	18,980	23	810
Women's footwear, except athletic	218	131	3,702	11,571	44	1,564
Women's handbags	32	19	773	11,666	4	139
Protected by import quotas						
Agriculture						
Dairy products	513	308	2,378	22,624	151	6,669
Peanuts	18	6	397	17,104[e]	5	170[f]
Sugar	548	329	2,261	21,810	170	7,493
Maritime	1,434	860	4,411	28,157	449	15,905

Protected by "voluntary" export restraints					
Apparel	10,851	6,511	152,583	12,436	2,443	70,256[g]
Textiles	1,773	1,064	16,203	16,640	440	15,558
Machine tools	169	101	1,556	27,102	25	894
Total	16,697	10,014	191,764	15,649[h]	4,039	129,814

a. This column represents the volume effect from liberalization, calculated using base-year prices.

b. Nonwage value added is assumed to be 60 percent of the change in domestic production for each category, except peanuts, where the nonwage value added is calculated as 35 percent (peanut shipments are calculated at the farm gate unlike dairy products and sugar, which are calculated at the processing plant). This figure is based on the overall average share of nonwage value added for the manufacturing sector.

c. The data refer to production workers.

d. This column is calculated as the residual change in domestic production divided by the average yearly earnings in ancillary industries, which is assumed to be $28,255 for manufacturing, and $22,674 for the farm sector (applied to frozen concentrated orange juice, dairy products, and sugar; for peanuts, see note f). The figure for the farm sector is a simple average of manufacturing earnings ($28,255) and farm sector earnings ($17,104), assuming that half of ancillary employees come from each sector. Note that the employment impact in ancillary industries includes any impact on nonproduction workers in the industry directly affected, as well as workers in upstream industries supplying inputs. Note also that these calculations overstate the potential impact on employment in ancillary industries because nonwage value added is not deducted from the residual.

e. This figure refers to the average yearly earnings for the entire farm sector.

f. Ancillary employment for the peanut crop refers to suppliers of agricultural inputs. The figure is based on average yearly earnings in manufacturing.

g. From the estimates in table 1.3, 16,203 of the ancillary jobs lost due to apparel liberalization would be in the textile sector; those jobs are excluded from this estimate so as to avoid double counting.

h. Weighted average.

Sources: US Department of Commerce, Statistical Abstract of the United States, 1992, tables 649, 1072, 1244; US Department of Labor, Supplement to Employment and Earnings, 1991.

Table 1.7 National welfare effects of liberalization, with terms-of-trade (TOT) effects, 1990

Product category	Tariff or equivalent, $(Pm-Pm'')/Pm''$ (percent)	Increase in world price, $(Pm'-Pm'')/Pm'$ (percent)	Decrease in import price, $(Pm-Pm')/Pm'$ (percent)	(A) Terms of trade loss (millions of dollars)	(B) Efficiency gain (millions of dollars)	(C) Transfer from foreigners (millions of dollars)	Net national welfare change $(B+C-A)$ (millions of dollars)
Cases with potential TOT losses							
Ball bearings	11.0	0.8	10.1	4	1	n.a.	−3
Benzenoid chemicals	9.0	2.5	6.2	49	5	n.a.	−44
Canned tuna	12.5	4.3	7.7	7	2	n.a.	−5
Ceramic articles	11.0	1.5	9.3	11	2	n.a.	−10
Ceramic tiles	19.0	1.5	17.2	7	2	n.a.	−5
Costume jewelry	9.0	3.6	5.0	21	2	n.a.	−20
Frozen concentrated orange juice	30.0	8.3	19.2	44	15	n.a.	−29
Glassware	11.0	3.7	6.9	33	4	n.a.	−29
Luggage	16.5	5.5	10.1	60	10	n.a.	−50
Polyethylene resins	12.0	6.6	4.6	36	3	n.a.	−33
Rubber footwear	20.0	3.9	15.4	28	7	n.a.	−21
Softwood lumber	6.5	2.4	3.9	68	4	n.a.	−64
Women's footwear, except athletic	10.0	1.9	7.9	57	7	n.a.	−50
Women's handbags	13.5	4.3	8.6	40	6	n.a.	−34
Dairy products	50.0	12.8	30.9	72	44	n.a.	−28
Subtotal	13.1[b]	3.5[b]	9.0[b]	538	112	0	−426

Cases where the transfer of
foreign rents offsets
potential TOT loss:[a]

Peanuts	50.0	27.7	8.5	negl.	negl.	negl.	negl.
Sugar	66.0	14.2	42.5	99	86	297	383
Apparel	69.8	12.9	47.9	2,413	2,301	5,411	7,712
Textiles	33.7	7.7	23.5	437	181	713	894
Machine tools	55.8	5.9	46.6	44	35	350	385
Subtotal	62.3[b]	11.7[b]	43.0[b]	2,993	2,603	6,771	9,374[c]
Total	45.8[b]	8.9[b]	31.6[b]	538[c]	2,715	6,771	8,948[c]

NB: Pm is the preliberalization US price for the imported good; Pm'' is the preliberalization world price (which equals $Pm/(1+t)$); and Pm' is the new equilibrium price after liberalization; see figure 2.3 in chapter 2. The methodology used in estimating the tariff equivalents in the quantitative restriction cases with terms-of-trade effects is described in chapter 2. Maritime is excluded from the terms-of-trade exercise because it is highly implausible that the Jones Act affects enough trade to have an impact on world shipping rates.

n.a. = not applicable.

a. In these cases, the theoretical terms-of-trade loss does not actually arise because we assumed that the foreign exporters capture the quota rents. This means that, with the import restriction in place, the foreign exporter sells into the US market at the higher US market price, Pm, rather than at the lower world price, Pm''. Thus, there is no actual terms-of-trade gain for the United States with the barrier in place and, consequently, no terms-of-trade loss when the barrier is lifted. Note, however, that, with liberalization, the United States does recapture the portion of the quota rents arising from the difference between Pm and Pm', the new equilibrium world price after liberalization; these gains are presented in the column labeled "transfer from foreigners." The entries in the terms-of-trade loss column represent the additional quota rents that the United States could theoretically capture if the government auctioned, or otherwise allocated to US citizens, the same quantity of import rights that are now assigned to foreign exporters. See chapter 2 for further details; see also Bergsten et al. (1987) for a discussion of how the allocation of quota rights affects the distribution of the quota rents.

b. Weighted average.

c. These totals exclude the cases in which the transfer of quota rents to foreigners obviates the potential terms-of-trade loss.

all the difference between the world price and the quota-restricted price.[16] Since the United States does not benefit from the trade barrier–induced reduction in the world price, it does not lose when the world price rises following liberalization.

A country may also experience a terms-of-trade loss from trade liberalization if exchange rate depreciation is necessary to correct any resulting trade deficit. Using estimates from the literature of aggregate elasticities of demand and supply for US exports and imports, Tarr and Morkre (1984, 26–27) derive a parameter, with a value of 0.038, that may be used to estimate the exchange rate aspects of the terms-of-trade effect. Assuming that the increase in the value of imports due to liberalization is not offset by decreased US imports in related sectors or increased US exports (for example, because of positive income effects among our trading partners or because of reciprocal liberalization by them), the outside estimate of the terms-of-trade loss in 1990 using the Tarr-Morkre parameter is around $200 million.[17]

A final caveat about the caveats is in order. All the estimates assume that liberalization is undertaken instantaneously and unilaterally. In practice, any reduction in trade barriers is likely to be gradual, spreading the impact over a number of years. Moreover, in reality, any liberalization would likely occur as part of a multilateral trade negotiation (such as the Uruguay Round), which would increase US exports as a result of concessions from other trading partners. Increased US exports would likely offset both direct and ancillary job losses, downward pressure on the dollar, and any other terms-of-trade effect, since prices for US exports should rise as a result of increased foreign demand.

---

16. See Bergsten, et al., 1987, for a description of how quota administration and market structure affect the distribution of the quota rents.

17. Readers should note that the induced increase in the *value* of imports to which the Tarr-Morkre parameter is applied, differs from the *volume* figure reported in table 1.2. The figure of $200 million is calculated using an estimated change in the *value* of imports following liberalization calculated as $PmQm - Pm'Qm'$ (using the notation defined in chapter 2). To get an idea of the *volume* change in imports following liberalization, the estimate of increased imports in table 1.2 uses constant prices and is calculated as $Pm'(Qm' - Qm)$.

2

A Computable Partial Equilibrium Model

This chapter outlines the simple comparative static framework used in this study for calculating the welfare effects of trade barriers.[1] The framework is similar to that found in Morkre and Tarr (1980) and Tarr and Morkre (1984); it is founded on a partial equilibrium analysis with four key assumptions:

- the domestic good and the imported good are imperfect substitutes;

- the supply schedule for the imported good is flat (perfectly elastic);[2]

- the supply schedule for the domestic good is upwardly sloped (less than perfectly elastic);

- all markets are perfectly competitive.

The effects of removing a trade barrier (either a tariff or a quota) are illustrated in figures 2.1 and 2.2. For example, elimination of a tariff lowers the price of the import in the domestic market from Pm to Pm' in figure 2.1. In figure 2.2, the decrease in the price of the imported good causes an inward shift in the demand curve for the domestic com-

---

1. This chapter was largely written and the computable equilibrium model designed by Peter Uimonen when he was a research assistant at IIE. Mr. Uimonen is currently an economist at the International Monetary Fund.

2. This assumption is relaxed for supplementary calculations presented in the addendum to this chapter.

Figure 2.1 Effects in the import market of removing a trade barrier

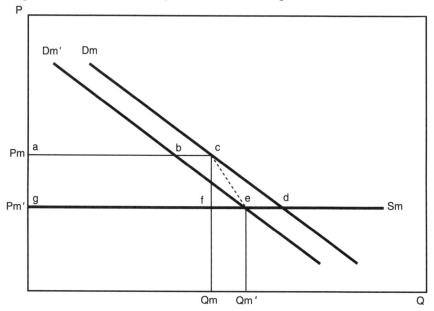

With the trade barrier in place, the price of the import in the protected market is *Pm*, and the quantity imported is *Qm*. Following liberalization, the price falls to *Pm'*, the world price. Then, responding to a lower price in the domestic market (see figure 2.2), the demand schedule for the import shifts from *Dm* to *Dm'*, and the quantity imported settles at *Qm'*.

modity from *Dd* to *Dd'*. This in turn leads to a decrease in the price of the domestic product from *Pd* to *Pd'*.

Returning to figure 2.1, the decrease in the domestic price causes the demand schedule for the imported good to shift from *Dm* to *Dm'*. When equilibrium is restored, prices of both the imported good and the domestic good are lower, output of the domestically produced good is also lower (by the difference between *Qd* and *Qd'*), and the quantity of imports is higher (by the difference between *Qm* and *Qm'*).[3]

Calculating the Welfare Effects of Trade Barriers

The changes in prices and quantities due to trade liberalization result in a gain of consumer surplus, both in the import market and the domestic market. Part of the gain arises because consumers now pay less for a

---

3. The same story could be told if the initial liberalization was to increase an import quota from *Qm* to *Qm'*. Then the system would work back to lower import prices.

Figure 2.2 Effects in the domestic market of removing a trade barrier

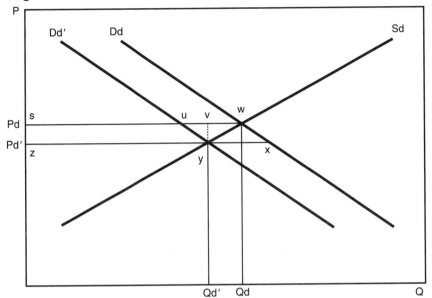

With the trade barrier in place, the price of the import-competing domestic product is *Pd*, and the quantity demanded is *Qd*. Following liberalization and the decline in the import price (see figure 2.1), demand for the domestic substitute falls, shifting the demand curve from *Dd* to *Dd'*, the quantity consumed falls to *Qd'*, and the price drops to *Pd'*.

good than they paid when supply was restricted. In addition, some consumers, who previously were priced out of the market entirely, will now enter the market. The consumer surplus gain due to liberalization, however, is partially offset by a loss in producer surplus in the market for the domestic substitute, where prices and output both fall.

If the trade restraint took the form of a tariff, then the revenue lost by the government would also partially offset the consumer gain. If instead a quantitative restraint (QR) was used, liberalization would elimi-nate the quota rents that previously went either to domestic importers or foreign exporters, or some combination of the two, depending both on how the QR was allocated and on the economic power of the market participants (see Bergsten et al. 1987). Finally, there will be an efficiency gain because the trade restraint resulted in a misallocation of resources. Before liberalization, the wedge created between the domestic price of the import and the world price caused a transfer of resources toward production of the import substitute and away from other sectors where those resources could have been used more efficiently.

The methodology used here to quantify these welfare effects is based on Morkre and Tarr (1980). Because the imported and domestic goods are imperfect substitutes, the total gain to consumers must be calculated as the sum of the consumer surplus gain in the two separate markets. Returning to figure 2.1, Morkre and Tarr estimate that the consumer surplus gain from liberalization in the import market is approximated by the area bounded by points $aceg$. This method of estimating the consumer gain in the import market follows from the analysis of Burns (1973) on the measurement of consumer surplus and gives an average of the consumer gains calculated separately from the two demand curves.[4] Using the old demand schedule (Dm) gives the area marked $acdg$ as the change in consumer surplus, while the new demand schedule (Dm') gives the area marked $abeg$. The difference between the two areas is shown by the parallelogram marked $bcde$. Line ce divides the area in half and gives the compromise consumer surplus change, area $aceg$. Area $aceg$ can be estimated by adding rectangle $acfg$ to triangle cef.

If the form of the protection is a tariff, the rectangular area $acfg$ represents a transfer from the government to consumers in the form of lost tariff revenues, and may be estimated as:

$$(Pm - Pm') \times (Qm) \tag{2.1}$$

The area of the triangle marked cef represents recovery of the deadweight efficiency loss, which may be estimated as:

$$(1/2) \times [(Pm - Pm') \times (Qm' - Qm)] \tag{2.2}$$

If quantitative restraints are used, and if all the quota rents previously have been captured by foreign exporters, then area $acfg$ is recovered by the domestic economy from foreign interests. In that case, the consumer gain in the import market, the sum of rectangle $acfg$ and triangle cef, will also equal the net national welfare gain. If both tariffs and quotas are imposed, the tariff equivalent of the quota is assumed to be the difference between the total decline in the import price ($Pm - Pm'$) and the price effect of the tariff.[5]

Turning next to the domestic effects in figure 2.2, the consumer welfare gain from lower domestic prices may be approximated by the area marked $swyz$. Area $swyz$ can be estimated by adding rectangle $svyz$ and triangle vwy. This amounts to:

$$(Pd - Pd') \times (Qd') + (1/2) \times [(Pd - Pd') \times (Qd - Qd')] \tag{2.3}$$

In the domestic market, the consumer surplus gain is just offset by the producer surplus loss.

---

4. See Jones (1993) for a mathematical proof of the validity of this method.

5. The price effect of the tariff is normally calculated as Pm' times the ad valorem tariff rate.

Applying the Model

In order to apply the analysis to particular cases, a simple computable equilibrium model was devised corresponding to the graphical analysis above. The form of the model chosen assumes that demand and supply relationships are not linear in absolute terms, but rather are linear in terms of their logarithms. This assumption enables the parameters associated with the price terms to be interpreted as elasticities.

In order to achieve this result, it is necessary to specify the underlying domestic demand and supply functions according to the following forms:

$$Qd = aPd^{Edd}Pm^{Edm} \qquad (2.4)$$

$$Qs = bPd^{Es} \qquad (2.5)$$

In equation 2.4, E_{dd} is the own-price elasticity of demand for the domestic commodity, while E_{dm} is the cross-price elasticity of demand for the domestic commodity with respect to the price of the imported commodity.[6] In equation 2.5, E_s is the own-price elasticity of the supply of the domestic good. Since the domestic commodity and the import are imperfect substitutes in this model, equilibrium in the domestic market requires that domestic demand equals domestic supply—that is, that Qd equals Qs.

Assuming that the supply of the import is perfectly elastic, the supply and demand equations in the import market are:

$$Qm = cPd^{Emd}Pm^{Emm} \qquad (2.6)$$

$$Pm = Pm''(1+t) \qquad (2.7)$$

In equation 2.6, E_{md} is the cross-price elasticity of demand for the imported commodity with respect to the price of the domestic commodity, while E_{mm} is the own-price elasticity of demand for the imported commodity. Equation 2.7 represents the assumption that the supply of the imported commodity is perfectly elastic, and, therefore, the world price, Pm'', which equals $Pm/(1+t)$, is the same no matter what the level of imports.

This system of demand and supply functions may be transformed into a system of linear relationships simply by taking the logarithms to the base e (shown by ln) of equations 2.4, 2.5, 2.6, and 2.7:

---

6. The own-price elasticity of demand for the domestic commodity, $E_{dd,}$ is defined as the percentage change in the quantity demanded for each 1 percent change in the price. Other own-price elasticities are defined in an analogous way. Own-price elasticities are normally negative (i.e., an increase in the price of the domestic good causes a decrease in demand for the domestic good). The cross-price elasticity of demand for the domestic commodity, $E_{dm,}$ is defined as the percentage change in the quantity of the domestic good demanded for each 1 percent change in the price of the imported good. Other cross-price elasticities are defined in a similar way. Cross-price elasticities are normally positive (i.e., an increase in the price of the imported good causes an increase in demand for the domestic good).

$$\ln Qd = \ln a + E_{dd}\ln Pd + E_{dm}\ln Pm \qquad (2.8)$$
$$\ln Qs = \ln b + E_s\ln Pd \qquad (2.9)$$
$$\ln Qm = \ln c + E_{md}\ln Pd + E_{mm}\ln Pm \qquad (2.10)$$
$$\ln Pm = \ln[Pm'' \, (1+t)] \qquad (2.11)$$

Estimating the effects of a change in trade protection using this system requires two basic steps. First, price and quantity data are used, together with estimates of the elasticity parameters, to solve equations 2.8, 2.9, and 2.10 for the unobservable constant terms, namely $\ln a$, $\ln b$, and $\ln c$. These terms represent the effects of other (unobserved) nonprice variables on the demand and supply functions. The crucial assumption in this step is that the base period for which the price and quantity data are collected may be considered an equilibrium period (i.e., a period in which it is reasonable to suppose that Qd is equal to Qs).

The second step is to use the estimates of the intercepts and the elasticity parameters, together with a separately estimated change in either the price or the quantity of the import due to a change in protection, to calculate a new equilibrium and, hence, the comparative-static welfare effects of the change.

Suppose, for example, that a tariff is eliminated. By invoking the assumption that $\ln Qd$ equals $\ln Qs$, equations 2.8 and 2.9 may be solved together to yield the new price of the domestic commodity as a function of the new import price:

$$\ln Pd' = (\ln a - \ln b)/(E_s - E_{dd}) + [E_{dm}/(E_s - E_{dd})] \times \ln Pm' \quad (2.12)$$

In equation 2.12, $\ln Pm'$ is represented by the previous (base period) import price (corresponding to Pm in figure 2.1) minus the change in the price induced by elimination of the tariff (corresponding to the difference between Pm and Pm' in figure 2.1). To facilitate computation, base period prices (inclusive of the tariff) are assumed equal to index values of 1.00; hence tariff changes can be represented in ad valorem terms where the ad valorem rate is applied to the world price without the tariff, Pm'. For example, elimination of a 15 percent tariff would mean that $\ln Pm'$ is equal to $\ln(0.87)$, i.e., to $\ln(1/1.15)$. The new import and domestic prices can then be substituted into equations 2.8, 2.9, and 2.10 to yield the new equilibrium quantities of imports and domestic output. The welfare effects of the tariff change may then be computed using expressions 2.1, 2.2, and 2.3.

The case where a quota is eliminated is more complicated. If the new quantity of imports, Qm', can be estimated, then equation 2.10 may be rearranged to express the new import price (after eliminating quota rents) as a function of both the new quantity imported and the new domestic price:

$$\ln Pm' = [\ln Qm' - \ln c - E_{md}\ln Pd']/E_{mm} \qquad (2.13)$$

Equations 2.12 and 2.13 may then be solved together to yield the two new prices: Pm' and Pd'. These, in turn, yield the output of the domestic commodity using equation 2.8. Once again, the comparative-static welfare effects of the change in protection may be estimated using the formulations described in expressions 2.1, 2.2, and 2.3.

In many cases, however, quantitative restrictions have been in place for so long that it is impossible to know what the free-trade level of imports might be. In those cases, it may be possible to estimate the price effect of the quota if data on prices in the world and domestic markets are available. This estimated "tariff equivalent" of the quota may then be used to calculate Pm', which in turn is inserted into equation 2.12 and used to calculate the other prices and quantities as in the tariff case.[7]

Computing Elasticities of Demand and Supply

Often values for some of the elasticity parameters needed for the model are not available in the literature. Estimates of cross-price elasticities, in particular, are rare. As outlined below, assumptions about the relationships among the parameters have been made as necessary to estimate unknown parameters based on the values that are available.

In some cases, an estimate of the price elasticity of aggregate demand for imports and the domestic good combined is available, while separate estimates for the two own-price elasticities of demand are not known. In order to facilitate computation, it is assumed that the demand structure is of the "constant elasticity of substitution" (CES) form. If the elasticity of substitution[8] between the two commodities is available, or can be estimated, estimates of the own-price elasticities of demand may be derived using the following equations:

$$E_{dd} = -\left[(1 - Sd) \times \acute{o} + (Sd \times E_{dt})\right] \tag{2.14}$$

$$E_{mm} = -\left[(1 - Sm) \times \acute{o} + (Sm \times E_{dt})\right] \tag{2.15}$$

where E_{dt} = price elasticity of total demand, $\acute{o}$ = elasticity of substitution between the domestic and imported goods (with both defined to be positive), Sd is the share by value of the domestic product in consump-

---

7. Tariff equivalents, rather than quantity changes, were estimated in the cases involving import quotas on dairy products, peanuts, and sugar, and the "voluntary" restraint agreements on textiles and apparel. Equation 2.13 was thus used only in the maritime, machine tool, and auto VER cases. The methods used to estimate the restrictive effects of QRs in these cases are discussed in appendix I.

8. The elasticity of substitution is defined as the percentage change in the ratio of quantity demanded of the imported good to the quantity demanded of the domestic good, for each 1 percent change in the price of the imported good relative to the price of the domestic good.

tion, and Sm is the share by value of imports in consumption (see Tarr 1990, 262, equation 16).[9]

Following a methodology developed by David Tarr (1990, 262, equation 17), if these own-price elasticities of demand and the elasticity of aggregate demand are known, the cross-price elasticities in the CES case may be calculated from:

$$E_{md} = [-Sd(E_{dt} + E_{dd})]/Sm \qquad (2.16)$$

$$E_{dm} = [-Sm(E_{dt} + E_{mm})]/Sd. \qquad (2.17)$$

An alternative methodology has been developed by Rousslang and Suomela (1985, 85). In many cases, the elasticity of aggregate demand is not available, but estimates of one or both of the own-price elasticities of demand are available in the literature. Using the Rousslang-Suomela method, the cross-elasticities may be derived as follows:

$$E_{md} = [(E_{mm} - E_{dd}) \times Vd]/(Vm - Vd) \qquad (2.18)$$

$$E_{dm} = [(E_{dd} - E_{mm}) \times Vm]/(Vd - Vm) \qquad (2.19)$$

where Vd is the value of domestic production, and Vm is the value of imports, c.i.f., duty-paid. These approximations assume there is little difference between the measured own-price elasticities of demand and the underlying compensated own-price elasticities, which would reflect the responsiveness of demand changes to relative price changes if consumers were compensated (or taxed) to offset the change in real incomes that result from the price change itself (Rousslang and Parker 1984; Leamer and Stern 1970, 65–66; Rousslang and Suomela 1985).

Finally, in many cases, the elasticity of supply also is not known. If a plausible value for the coefficient of price response, $(Pd - Pd')/(Pm - Pm')$, can be determined, then the elasticity of supply for the domestic good may be estimated by:

$$E_s = E_{dd} + E_{dm}/\theta \qquad (2.20)$$

where θ is the coefficient of price response (Cline 1990, 362, equation 19).

Incorporating Terms-of-Trade Effects[10]

The basic model described above assumes that the country imposing the trade barrier cannot affect prices in world markets. If the country

---

9. In cases where the elasticity of substitution is not available in the literature, the estimated value for the elasticity of substitution between imported and domestically produced sugar, a homogeneous good, is used as the baseline for our "guesstimates" in the cases. The value 5 is the "best" estimate offered by both the Federal Trade Commission (1990, 18–19) and the US International Trade Commission (1990, E-4) for sugar. This is the largest elasticity of substitution estimate offered by either source for a variety of agricultural and, in the FTC report, other products.

10. The authors thank Chang-tai Hsieh for assistance in the preparation of this section.

Figure 2.3 Import market with terms of trade effect

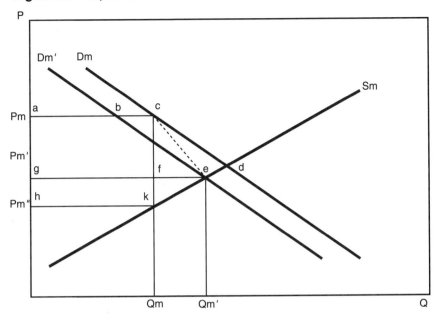

With the trade barrier in place, the price of the import in the protected market is *Pm*, the world price is *Pm"*, and the quantity demanded is *Qm*. Following liberalization, the price of the import in the domestic market falls and the world price rises; the result is a new world price, *Pm'*. Then, responding to a lower price in the domestic market (see figure 2.2), the demand schedule for the import shifts from *Dm* to *Dm'*, and the quantity imported settles at *Qm'*. Note that *Pm"* is equal to *Pm/(1 + t)*, where *t* is the ad valorem tariff or tariff equivalent.

accounts for a large enough share of the world market for particular products, however, the reduction in demand resulting from the imposition of a tariff or quota may be large enough to force foreign exporters to lower prices, thus forcing foreign producers to share some of the cost of the tariff. This "large-country assumption" is represented in figure 2.3 by an upwardly sloping supply curve. Previously, in figure 2.1, the supply curve for imports was flat, reflecting the assumption of perfectly elastic foreign supply.

In figure 2.3, with the trade barrier in place, the initial price in the import market is *Pm*; the preliberalization world price is *Pm"*, which equals *Pm/(1 + t)*, where *t* is the tariff (or tariff equivalent if the restriction is a quota); and *Qm* is the level of imports. If the trade barrier is lifted, and after adjustments have been made in the domestic market (as described above), the new equilibrium will settle at the intersection of *Sm* and the new demand curve, *Dm'*; the new volume of imports will be *Qm'* and the new price will be *Pm'*. Note that *Pm'* is lower than the preliberalization price in the protected home market for imports, *Pm*, but is higher than the preliberalization world price, *Pm"*.

As before, the consumer surplus gain from liberalization is area *aceg*, and the efficiency gain is the area of triangle *cef*. In this case, however, the tariff revenue or quota rent generated by the restriction is the area *ackh*, including the rectangle *gfkh*, which represents the terms-of-trade loss resulting from the increase in the world price (from Pm'' to Pm') after liberalization. Although it represents a loss either to the importing-country government in the case of a tariff or to quota license holders, area *gfkh* is not included in the measure of consumer surplus lost because it is not a cost borne by domestic consumers. The triangle marked *fek* is another deadweight loss, but it affects foreign suppliers, not domestic consumers of the imported good, and thus is not included in the calculation of the consumer surplus gain from liberalization.

In this case, therefore, the tariff revenue or quota rent generated, area *ackh*, may be measured as: $(Pm - Pm'') \times Qm$. The efficiency gain from liberalization, triangle *cef*, is calculated as before, $[1/2 \times (Pm - Pm') \times (Qm' - Qm)]$, and the terms-of-trade loss from liberalization may be measured as $(Pm' - Pm'') \times Qm$. The consumer surplus gain then may be calculated as the sum of the tariff revenue (or quota rent), rectangle *ackh*, plus the efficiency gain, triangle *cef*, minus the terms-of-trade loss, rectangle *gfkh*, or:

$$[Pm - Pm''] \times Qm + (1/2) \times [(Pm - Pm') \times (Qm - Qm')]$$
$$- [Pm' - Pm'')] \times Qm \qquad (2.21)$$

Calculation of the consumer surplus gain in the domestic market is the same as in the base case with no terms-of-trade effects.

Introduction of a terms-of-trade effect also requires modification of the computable equilibrium model used in calculating the effects of trade barriers. Because the supply curve for imports is no longer perfectly elastic, a new equation, 11a, is needed to represent the foreign supply function:

$$\ln Qsm = \ln d + E_{sm} \ln Pm'' \qquad (2.11a)$$

where Qsm represents the supply of imports and E_{sm} is the elasticity of supply of imports. Pm'' is the world price of the imported good with the trade barrier in place (see figure 2.3). Equations 2.8 through 2.10, representing demand and supply for the domestic good, and demand for the imported good, remain the same.

Previously, the new equilibrium price, Pm', could be estimated knowing Pm and the ad valorem tariff; now Pm' must be solved for simultaneously with Pd'.

In the case of eliminating a tariff, equations 2.10 and 2.11a may be solved together to yield the new import price as a function of the new domestic price:

$$\ln Pm' = (\ln c - \ln d)/(E_{sm} - E_{mm}) + [E_{md}/(E_{sm} - E_{mm})] \times \ln Pd' \quad (2.22)$$

Equations 2.12 and 2.22 can be solved together to yield the new import and domestic prices. Equations 2.8 and 2.10 may then be used with the new prices to estimate the new import and domestic quantities, Qm' and Qd'.

In the case of eliminating a quota, when the new import quantity Qm' can be determined exogenously on the basis of a side calculation, equations 2.12 and 2.13 may be solved together as in the base case to yield the new domestic and import prices; equation 2.8 can then be used to yield the new domestic quantity, Qd'. Determining the terms-of-trade effect, however, requires additional steps. Because t, the tariff equivalent of the quota, is not known, the preliberalization world price, Pm'', also is not known. However, once the new import price, Pm' (equal to Pm'' in the postliberalization equilibrium), is derived from solving equations 2.12 and 2.13, the values of Pm' and Qm' can be used in equation 2.11a, together with the assumed value of Esm, to calculate a value for $\ln d$ (recall that the new demand for imports, Qm', is assumed equal to the new supply of imports, Qsm'). The value of $\ln Pm''$ can then be calculated by substituting the preliberalization level of imports, Qm, and the just-calculated $\ln d$ into equation 2.11a and solving as follows:

$$\ln Pm'' = (\ln Qm - \ln d)/E_{sm} \qquad (2.23)$$

Finally, the value of t can be calculated from Pm and Pm'' (equal to $Pm/(1+t)$).

In cases where Qm' cannot be estimated, it may be possible to calculate the price effect of the quota. Depending on the assumptions made, estimates of the tariff equivalents of quotas may be used to derive either the import price after liberalization, Pm', or the preliberalization world price, Pm''. For example, the estimate of the tariff equivalents of the QRs on textiles and apparel used in the US case (see appendix I) are estimated using a model that assumes perfectly elastic foreign supply. In that case, in estimating the terms-of-trade effect, it seems most appropriate to treat the tariff equivalent as measuring the difference between Pm and Pm'; in other words, it is assumed that the "tariff equivalent" does not capture the entire price effect of the quota if possible terms-of-trade effects on world prices are taken into account. In the textile and apparel cases, the estimates of "tariff equivalents" are used to calculate a new Pm', and then equations 2.8, 2.10, and 2.12 may be used as before to calculate the new import quantity and the new domestic price and quantity. The value of $\ln d$ and the preliberalization world price, Pm'', may then be calculated as in the quota cases, where Qm' is known from a side calculation.

In other cases—for example, dairy products, peanuts, and sugar—it is possible to get data on world prices exclusive of any quota rents that may be captured by foreign exporters. In these cases, a tariff equivalent derived by comparing prices for the domestic good with world prices is assumed not to reflect terms-of-trade effects in the base case but is assumed to reflect terms-of-trade effects here. An estimate of a tariff equivalent thus derived may be used to calculate Pm''. The new equilibrium prices and quantities for imported and domestic goods may then be calculated using equations 2.8, 2.10, 2.12, and 2.22 as described above for the tariff cases.

Chapter References

Bergsten, C. Fred, Kimberly A. Elliott, Jeffrey J. Schott, and Wendy E. Takacs. 1987. *Auction Quotas and United States Trade Policy.* POLICY ANALYSES IN INTERNATIONAL ECONOMICS 19. Washington: Institute for International Economics.

Burns, Michael E. 1973. "A Note on the Concept and Measure of Consumer's Surplus." *American Economic Review* 63, no. 3: 335–44.

Cline, William R. 1990. *The Future of World Trade in Textiles and Apparel.* Washington: Institute for International Economics.

Cline, William R. 1989. *United States External Adjustment and the World Economy.* Washington: Institute for International Economics.

Destler, I. M. 1992. *American Trade Politics.* Washington: Institute for International Economics.

Federal Trade Commission. 1990. *Effects of U.S. Import Restraints on Agricultural and Other Products: General Equilibrium Results.* Washington: FTC Bureau of Economics (May).

Finger, J. Michael, ed. 1993. *Antidumping: How It Works and Who Gets Hurt.* Ann Arbor: The University of Michigan Press.

General Agreement on Tariffs and Trade. 1993. *Trade, the Uruguay Round and the Consumer.* Geneva: GATT.

Hufbauer, Gary Clyde, Diane T. Berliner, and Kimberly Ann Elliott. 1986. *Trade Protection in the United States: 31 Case Studies.* Washington: Institute for International Economics.

Hufbauer, Gary Clyde, and Howard F. Rosen. 1986. *Trade Policy for Troubled Industries.* POLICY ANALYSES IN INTERNATIONAL ECONOMICS 15. Washington: Institute for International Economics.

Jones, Michael. 1993. "The Geometry of Protectionism in the Imperfect Substitutes Model: A Reminder." *Southern Economic Journal* 60 (July): 235–38.

Katz, Lawrence F., and Lawrence H. Summers. 1989. "Industry Rents: Evidence and Implications." *Brooking Papers on Economic Activitiy: Microeconomics 1989.* Washington: Brookings Institution.

Leamer, Edward, and Robert Stern. 1970. *Quantitative International Economics.* Chicago: Aldine Publishing Co.

de Melo, Jaime, and David Tarr. 1992. *A General Equilibrium Analysis of US Foreign Trade Policy.* Cambridge, MA: MIT Press.

Morkre, Morris, and David G. Tarr. 1980. *Effects of Restrictions on United States Imports: Five Case Studies and Theory*. Bureau of Economics Staff Report. Washington: Federal Trade Commission (June).

Organization for Economic Cooperation and Development. 1993. *Agricultural Policies, Market and Trade: Monitoring and Outlook 1993*. Paris: OECD.

Podgursky, Michael. 1992. "The Industrial Structure of Job Displacement: 1979–1989." *Monthly Labor Review*, September.

Richardson, J. David. 1989. "Empirical Research on Trade Liberalization with Imperfect Competition: A Survey." *Statistics Working Papers* no. 58. Geneva: Organization for Economic Cooperation and Development.

Rousslang, Donald, and Stephen Parker. 1984. "Cross-Price Elasticities of U.S. Import Demand." *Review of Economics and Statistics*. 66 (August): 518–23.

Rousslang, Donald, and John Suomela. 1985. "Calculating the Consumer and Net Welfare Costs of Import Relief." Staff Research Study no. 15. Washington: US International Trade Commission.

Tarr, David G. 1990. "A Modified Cournot Aggregation Condition for Obtaining Estimates of Cross-Elasticities of Demand." *Eastern Economic Journal* 16, no. 3 (July-September): 257–64.

Tarr, David G., and Morris Morkre. 1984. *Aggregate Costs to the United States of Tariffs and Quotas on Imports: General Tariff Cuts and Removal of Quotas on Automobiles, Steel, Sugar, and Textiles*. Bureau of Economics Staff Report. Washington: Federal Trade Commission. (December).

US International Trade Commission. 1993. *The Economic Effects of Significant US Import Restraints*. USITC Publication 2699. Washington: USITC (November).

US International Trade Commission. 1990. *The Economic Effects of Significant U.S. Import Restraints, Phase II: Agricultural Products and Natural Resources*. USITC Pub. 2314. Washington: USITC (September).

US International Trade Commission. 1989a. *The Economic Effects of Significant U.S. Import Restraints, Phase I: Manufacturing*. USITC Pub. 2222. Washington: USITC (October).

US International Trade Commission. 1989b. *The Effects of the Voluntary Restraint Agreements on U.S. Steel-Consuming Industries*. USITC Pub. 2182. Washington: USITC (May).

21 Cases in Effect
in 1990

Ball Bearings

The Tariff Act of 1930 (known as Smoot-Hawley) placed a tariff of 45 percent plus 10 cents per pound on ball and roller bearings. Negotiated trade concessions in the 1950s eventually reduced this rate to 3.4 cents per pound plus 15 percent ad valorem. The Kennedy Round of multilateral trade negotiations further reduced this rate to 1.7 cents per pound plus 7.5 percent ad valorem by 1972. Shortly thereafter, however, certain ball bearings received five years of import relief in the form of higher tariffs under the escape clause (see Hufbauer, Berliner, and Elliott 1986).

The escape clause duties on ball bearings expired in 1978. The duty rate on ball bearings without integral shafts (HTS 84821050) was unaffected by multilateral trade negotiations during the Tokyo Round, and in 1980 the rate was changed to the current ad valorem rate of 11 percent. The rate on other ball bearings with integral shafts was lowered eventually to an ad valorem rate of 4.2 percent and on roller bearings to 6.5 percent.

Effects of eliminating the tariff
(millions of dollars unless noted)

Consumer surplus gain	64
Producer surplus loss	13
Tariff revenue loss	50
Efficiency gain	1
Employment loss (number of workers)	146

Base-year data (1990)		Postliberalization estimates	
Import price (Pm) (dollars/pound)	1.47	Import price (Pm') (dollars/pound)	1.32
Import volume (Qm) (million pounds)	331	Import volume (Qm') (million pounds)	340
Domestic price[a] (Pd) (dollars/pound)	3.33	Domestic price (Pd') (dollars/pound)	3.30
Domestic output (Qd) (million pounds)	416	Domestic output (Qd') (million pounds)	412
Employment (production workers)	15,000	Employment (production workers)	14,854

PARAMETERS

Elasticities		Constants		Price effect of barrier	
E_{dd}	−0.10	lna	6.11	Average ad valorem	11.0
E_{dm}	0.10	lnb	4.83	tariff (percent)	
E_s	1.00	lnc	5.57		
E_{mm}	−0.28				
E_{md}	0.28				
θ	0.1				

a. Assumes that the unit value for ball bearings without integral shafts is the same as for all ball bearings (SIC 35621).

Sources: USITC Office of Industry, personal communication; *Census Bureau, Current Industrial Reports;* Hufbauer, Berliner, and Elliott 1986 (for E_{dd}).

Benzenoid Chemicals (SIC 2865)

Under the Tariff Act of 1922 (Fordney-McCumber), imports of benzenoid chemicals and their products were divided into two categories. "Competitive" imports were subject to high ad valorem tariffs and the American Selling Price (ASP) system of customs valuation, under which tariffs were calculated by applying the ad valorem rate to the wholesale price of a like or competitive domestic product rather than the export price in the country of origin, as is usually done. "Noncompetitive" imports were subject to somewhat lower ad valorem tariffs and the usual customs valuation. The average duty under the ASP valuation system on "competitive" imports in 1964 was 40 percent; this was equivalent to over 65 percent under the usual valuation system. The ASP system was finally terminated as a result of concessions in the Tokyo Round, which also provided for a series of staged tariff reductions on all benzenoid chemicals and products. Temporary duty suspensions and the conversion to the Harmonized Tariff System (HTS) of classification may have reduced average rates to a small degree (*National Journal*, 10 July 1993, 1756). However, after the Tokyo Round cuts and the HTS were fully implemented, the average tariff on certain benzenoid chemicals was still a relatively high figure, about 9.0 percent.

Effects of eliminating the tariff
(millions of dollars unless noted)

Consumer surplus gain	309
Producer surplus loss	127
Tariff revenue loss	172
Efficiency gain	10
Employment loss (number of workers)	216

Base-year data (1990)

		Postliberalization estimates	
Import price[a] (Pm) (index)	1.00	Import price (Pm') (index)	0.92
Import volume (Qm) (millions of dollars)	2,057	Import volume (Qm') (millions of dollars)	2,299
Domestic price[a] (Pd) (index)	1.00	Domestic price (Pd') (index)	0.99
Domestic output (Qd) (millions of dollars)	14,763	Domestic output (Qd') (millions of dollars)	14,533
Employment (production workers)	13,900	Employment (production workers)	13,684

PARAMETERS

Elasticities		Constants		Price effect of barrier	
E_{dd}	−0.20	lna	9.60	Average ad valorem tariff (percent)	9.0
E_{dm}	0.20	lnb	9.60		
E_s	1.80	lnc	7.63		
E_{mm}	−1.42				
E_{md}	1.42				
θ	0.1				

a. Since SIC 2865 contains hundreds of chemicals and products, some using different units of measure, data on the aggregate volume of products are not available. Instead, the value of shipments and imports must be used in place of the volumes, and an index is used for the prices.

Sources: Census Bureau, IM 175; *Annual Survey of Manufactures;* Hufbauer, Berliner, and Elliott 1986 (for E_{mm}).

Canned Tuna

Under Smoot-Hawley, the tariff on canned tuna in oil was originally 30 percent ad valorem. In 1934, it was raised to 45 percent, which induced a shift away from canned tuna packed in oil to tuna packed in water, dutiable at 15.5 percent. In 1955, the rate on tuna in oil was reduced to its current rate of 35 percent. The following year, pursuant to an agreement with Japan, a tariff-rate quota was established for tuna packed in water that set a rate of 12.5 percent for imports up to a level equal to 20 percent of the previous year's domestic US pack, and 25 percent above that level. These rates for tuna packed in water were lowered during the Kennedy Round to 6 and 12.5 percent, respectively. As a result of the differential between the duties for tuna packed in water and in oil, 98 percent of imported canned tuna today is packed in water.

Calculation of Tariff Equivalent and Elasticities

The ad valorem tariff, based on duties collected, averaged 10.5 percent in the late 1980s. Since the volume of imports has been well above the quota level in recent years, however, we assume that the over-quota tariff of 12.5 percent sets the price for all imports. The elasticity calculations are based on the US International Trade Commission's estimate of the elasticity of total demand of -0.5 (USITC 2339, 6-3) and an assumed elasticity of substitution between the domestic and imported products of 3. Although imported and domestically produced canned tuna might seem to be close substitutes, a somewhat lower, intermediate value is chosen because a larger proportion of the domestic good is white-meat tuna, while most imports are light-meat tuna.

Effects of eliminating the tariff-rate quota
(millions of dollars unless noted)

Consumer surplus gain	73
Producer surplus loss	31
Tariff revenue loss	31
Quota rent gain	6
Efficiency gain	4
Employment loss (number of workers)	390

Base-year data (1990)		Postliberalization estimates	
Import price (Pm) (dollars/pound)	1.19	Import price (Pm') (dollars/pound)	1.06
Import volume (Qm) (millions of pounds)	284	Import volume (Qm') (millions of pounds)	348
Domestic price (Pd) (dollars/pound)	1.56	Domestic price (Pd') (dollars/pound)	1.50
Domestic output (Qd) (millions of pounds)	579	Domestic output (Qd') (millions of pounds)	558
Employment (processing) (production workers, 1989)	11,000	Employment (production workers)	10,610

PARAMETERS

Elasticities		Constants		Price effects of barrier	
E_{dd}	−1.18	lna	6.77	Average ad valorem tariff (percent)	10.5
E_{dm}	0.68	lnb	5.92		
E_s	1.00	lnc	5.24		
E_{mm}	−2.33			Tariff equivalent of quota (percent)	2.0
E_{md}	1.84				
θ	0.3			Total tariff equivalent assumed eliminated	12.5

Sources: Census Bureau, *National Trade Databank;* National Oceanic and Atmospheric Administration; USITC Pub. No. 2339.

Ceramic Articles

Under Smoot-Hawley, tariffs on undecorated chinaware were 10 cents per dozen pieces plus 60 percent ad valorem; tariffs on decorated chinaware were 10 cents per dozen plus 70 percent ad valorem. Before the Kennedy Round, duties on chinaware (SIC 3262) ranged from 35 percent ad valorem for bone chinaware to 10 cents per dozen plus 60 percent ad valorem for other chinaware. As a result of the tariff reduction negotiations during the Kennedy Round, the duties on chinaware declined to 17.5 percent (bone) and to 10 cents per dozen plus 55 percent ad valorem (other). The Tokyo Round further reduced these tariffs, and they now range from 8 to 35 percent.

Smoot-Hawley tariffs on earthenware (SIC 3263) were 50 to 55 percent. Before the Kennedy Round, duties ranged from 10 cents per dozen plus 21 percent ad valorem to 10 cents per dozen plus 40 percent ad valorem. The Kennedy Round lowered these rates to 5 percent per dozen plus 10.5 percent ad valorem and 10 cents per dozen plus 21 percent ad valorem. After the Tokyo Round cuts, these duties ranged from 4.5 percent to 35 percent.

Effects of eliminating the tariff
(millions of dollars unless noted)

Consumer surplus gain	102
Producer surplus loss	18
Tariff revenue loss	81
Efficiency gain	2
Employment loss (number of workers)	418

Base-year data (1990)		**Postliberalization estimates**	
Import price[a] (Pm) (index)	1.00	Import price (Pm') (index)	0.90
Import volume (Qm) (millions of dollars)	819	Import volume (Qm') (millions of dollars)	864
Domestic price (Pd) (index)	1.00	Domestic price (Pd') (index)	0.95
Domestic output (Qd) (millions of dollars)	371	Domestic output (Qd') (millions of dollars)	333
Employment (production workers)	4,100	Employment (production workers)	3,682

PARAMETERS

Elasticities		**Constants**		**Price effect of barrier**	
E_{dd}	−2.27	lna	5.92	Average ad valorem tariff (percent)	11.0
E_{dm}	2.27	lnb	5.92		
E_s	2.00	lnc	6.71		
E_{mm}	−1.03				
E_{md}	1.00				
θ	0.5				

a. Since SIC codes 3262 and 3263 contain hundreds of products, data on the aggregate volume of products are not available. Instead, the value of shipments and imports must be used in place of the volumes, and an index is used for the prices.

Sources: Census Bureau, IM 175; *Annual Survey of Manufacturers;* Bureau of Labor Statistics, *Supplement to Employment and Earnings*; USITC (1989) Pub. No. 2222 (for E_{mm}).

Ceramic Floor and Wall Tile

When the Tariff Schedule for the United States (TSUS) was instituted in 1963, ceramic tiles (SIC 3253) were divided into three categories, and the Smoot-Hawley tariffs on each were significantly reduced, from 55 to 24.5 percent ad valorem on mosaic tiles, from 50 to 22.5 percent ad valorem on glazed nonmosaic tiles, and from 50 to 24 percent ad valorem on unglazed nonmosaic tiles. These tariffs were further reduced in the Tokyo Round (1979) to 20 percent ad valorem on mosaic tiles and unglazed nonmosaic tiles and 19 percent ad valorem on glazed nonmosaic tiles. The Tokyo Round also designated certain small or irregularly shaped mosaic tiles from Colombia, Malaysia, Guatemala, and Honduras as eligible articles under the Generalized System of Preferences.

Effects of eliminating the tariff
(millions of dollars unless noted)

Consumer surplus gain	139
Producer surplus loss	45
Tariff revenue loss	92
Efficiency gain	2
Employment loss (number of workers)	347

Base-year data (1990)		Postliberalization estimates	
Import price (Pm) (dollars/square foot)	1.01	Import price (Pm') (dollars/square foot)	0.85
Import volume (Qm) (millions of square feet)	572	Import volume (Qm') (millions of square feet)	601
Domestic price (Pd) (dollars/square foot)	1.28	Domestic price (Pd') (dollars/square foot)	1.19
Domestic output (Qd) (millions of square feet)	509	Domestic output (Qd') (millions of square feet)	487
Employment (production workers)	8,100	Employment (production workers)	7,753

PARAMETERS

Elasticities		Constants		Price effect of barrier	
E_{dd}	−0.44	lna	6.34	Average ad valorem tariff (percent)	19.0
E_{dm}	0.44	lnb	6.08		
E_s	0.60	lnc	6.23		
E_{mm}	−0.50				
E_{md}	0.50				
θ	0.4				

Sources: Census Bureau, IM 175; International Trade Administration, *The Industrial Outlook;* Washington Economic Research Consultants 1985 (for E_{mm}).

Costume Jewelry

The Smoot-Hawley rates on costume jewelry (SIC 3961) were between 45 and 55 percent for most articles and 15 percent for religious articles, although trade in the latter was small. The Kennedy Round of trade liberalization negotiations lowered these rates to a range of 10 to 35 percent. During the 1970s, duty rates on most imported costume jewelry ranged from 27.5 to 35 percent. The Tokyo Round further reduced these rates to a range of 6 to 14 percent, with the majority of imported costume jewelry charged a duty of 11 percent in 1988. None of the leading costume jewelry suppliers (South Korea, Taiwan, Austria, and China) are currently eligible for duty-free tariff treatment under the Generalized System of Preferences.

Effects of eliminating the tariff
(millions of dollars unless noted)

Consumer surplus gain	103
Producer surplus loss	46
Tariff revenue loss	51
Efficiency gain	5
Employment loss (number of workers)	1,067

Base-year data (1990)		Postliberalization estimates	
Import price[a] (Pm) (index)	1.00	Import price (Pm') (index)	0.92
Import volume (Qm) (millions of dollars)	621	Import volume (Qm') (millions of dollars)	754
Domestic price (Pd) (index)	1.00	Domestic price (Pd') (index)	0.97
Domestic output (Qd) (millions of dollars)	1,417	Domestic output (Qd') (millions of dollars)	1,302
Employment (production workers)	13,100	Employment (production workers)	12,033

PARAMETERS

Elasticities		Constants		Price effect of barrier	
E_{dd}	−1.65	lna	7.26	Average ad valorem tariff (percent)	9.0
E_{dm}	1.65	lnb	7.26		
E_s	2.45	lnc	6.43		
E_{mm}	−3.77				
E_{md}	3.77				
θ	0.4				

a. Since SIC 3961 contains many products, data on the aggregate volume of products are not available. Instead, the value of shipments and imports must be used in place of the volumes, and an index is used for the prices.

Sources: Census Bureau, IM 175; International Trade Administration, *Industrial Outlook;* USITC (1989) Pub. No. 2222 (for E_{mm}).

Frozen Concentrated Orange Juice

Pursuant to an agreement with Brazil in 1948, the Smoot-Hawley duty on frozen concentrated orange juice (FCOJ) was halved to 35 cents per gallon. Unconcentrated juice had a much lower tariff of 20 percent ad valorem. The Trade and Tariff Act of 1984 closed the "loophole" for unconcentrated juice by raising the duty on reconstituted juice with a concentration ratio higher than 1.5 (concentrate vs. diluted juice) to 35 cents per gallon. Only juice with a lower concentration retains the 20 percent duty for unconcentrated orange juice. The only exception to these rates (prior to the implementation of the North American Free Trade Agreement) is imports from Caribbean Basin Initiative countries, which are eligible for duty-free entry.

Effects of eliminating the tariff
(millions of dollars unless noted)

Consumer surplus gain	281
Producer surplus loss	101
Tariff revenue loss	145
Efficiency gain	35
Employment loss (number of workers)	609

Base-year data (average 1988-91)		Postliberalization estimates	
Import price (Pm) (dollars/gallon)	1.59	Import price (Pm') (dollars/gallon)	1.22
Import volume (Qm) (million gallons)	393	Import volume (Qm') (million gallons)	583
Domestic price[a] (Pd) (dollars/gallon)	1.78	Domestic price (Pd') (dollars/gallon)	1.66
Domestic output (Qd) (million gallons)	854	Domestic output (Qd') (million gallons)	797
Employment[b] (processing) (production workers)	8,880	Employment (production workers)	8,271

PARAMETERS

Elasticities[c]		Constants		Price effect of barrier	
E_{dd}	−1.05	lna	7.10	Average ad valorem tariff (percent)	30.0
E_{dm}	0.55	lnb	6.18		
E_s	1.00	lnc	6.05		
E_{mm}	−1.85				
E_{md}	1.35				
θ	0.3				

a. Assumed the same as for exports.

b. Assumes that the proportion of workers in SIC 2037 (processed foods) accounted for by FCOJ is the same as FCOJ's share of the total value of shipments by producers in category SIC 2037 (BLS; *The Industrial Outlook*).

c. The elasticity calculations are based on estimates by the USITC of the elasticities of aggregate demand (−0.5) and of substitution between the domestic and imported products (2.4) (Pub. No. 1623).

Sources: Census Bureau, *National Trade Databank;* USDA, 1992, *Horticultural Products Review;* Census Bureau, FT 447; USITC (1984) Pub. No. 1623.

Glass and Glassware (Pressed and Blown)

SIC 3229 includes a wide variety of glass products, with Smoot-Hawley tariffs ranging from 50 to 85 percent ad valorem for illuminating glassware, household glassware, and laboratory glassware, and from 20 to 40 percent ad valorem for bulbs, lenses, and tubing. As a result of the Tokyo Round, tariffs on illuminating glassware, Christmas ornaments, and other miscellaneous glassware were reduced to the current range of 2.4 to 15 percent ad valorem. The Tokyo Round also reduced the tariffs on household glassware to a range of 6 to 38 percent ad valorem, with an average of about 13 percent ad valorem by the time the tariff cuts were fully implemented in 1987.

Effects of eliminating the tariff
(millions of dollars unless noted)

Consumer surplus gain	266
Producer surplus loss	162
Tariff revenue loss	95
Efficiency gain	9
Employment loss (number of workers)	1,477

Base-year data (1990)		**Postliberalization estimates**	
Import price[a] (Pm) (index)	1.00	Import price (Pm') (index)	0.90
Import volume (Qm) (millions of dollars)	949	Import volume (Qm') (millions of dollars)	1,133
Domestic price[a] (Pd) (index)	1.00	Domestic price (Pd') (index)	0.96
Domestic output (Qd) (millions of dollars)	3,898	Domestic output (Qd') (millions of dollars)	3,733
Employment (production workers)	34,800	Employment (production workers)	33,323

PARAMETERS

Elasticities		Constants		Price effect of barrier	
E_{dd}	−0.70	lna	8.27	Average ad valorem tariff (percent)	11.0
E_{dm}	0.70	lnb	8.27		
E_s	1.00	lnc	6.86		
E_{mm}	−2.86				
E_{md}	2.86				
θ	0.4				

a. Since SIC 3229 is a miscellaneous category of glass products with different units of measure, data on the aggregate volume of these products are not available. Instead, the value of shipments and imports must be used in place of the volumes, and an index is used for the prices.

Sources: Census Bureau, IM 175; *Annual Survey of Manufactures*; Bureau of Labor Statistics; USITC (1989) Pub. No. 2222 (for E_{mm}).

Luggage (SIC 3161)

The Smoot-Hawley tariff rate for leather luggage was 35 percent. The rates for reptile hide and other leather luggage were reduced to 10 and 8.5 percent, respectively, in the Kennedy Round and to 5.3 and 8 percent, respectively, in the Tokyo Round. After conversion to the Harmonized Tariff System (HTS) in 1989, the duty on reptile leather was eliminated, and the duty on other leather was subdivided into two categories dutiable at 8 and 6.8 percent.

The Smoot-Hawley rate on nonleather luggage, which includes musical instrument cases, sports bags, attaché cases, etc., ranged from 35 to 90 percent. For most luggage made of textiles, the rate was 40 to 65 percent. The rate for most luggage made of plastic was 45 percent. The rate for nonleather luggage was lowered to between 6.5 and 21 percent in the Kennedy Round, while the duty on plastic luggage remained unchanged. The Tokyo Round further lowered tariffs only on products with small trade volumes, and in 1984, bilateral quotas under the Multi-Fiber Arrangement (MFA) were established for luggage made of textiles.[1]

---

1. For purposes of this case, it is assumed that the quotas are not binding and that only the tariffs restrict imports of luggage.

Effects of eliminating the tariff
(millions of dollars unless noted)

Consumer surplus gain	211
Producer surplus loss	16
Tariff revenue loss	169
Efficiency gain	26
Employment loss (number of workers)	226

Base-year data (1990)		Postliberalization estimates	
Import price (Pm) (dollars/unit)	4.34	Import price (Pm') (dollars/unit)	3.73
Import volume (Qm) (millions of units)	277	Import volume (Qm') (millions of units)	362
Domestic price[a] (Pd) (dollars/unit)	24.52	Domestic price (Pd') (dollars/unit)	24.15
Domestic output (Qd) (millions of units)	43	Domestic output (Qd') (millions of units)	42
Employment (production workers)	7,500	Employment (production workers)	7,274

PARAMETERS

Elasticities		Constants		Price effect of barrier	
E_{dd}	−2.06	lna	9.75	Average ad valorem	16.5
E_{dm}	0.41	lnb	−2.64	tariff (percent)	
E_s	2.00	lnc	6.60		
E_{mm}	−1.82				
E_{md}	0.53				
θ	0.1				

a. The *Current Industrial Report* reports volume and value of shipments for firms accounting for two-thirds of all firms in the industry. The unit value for the industry as a whole is assumed to be the same as that estimated from the *CIR* and is divided into the value of industry shipments as reported in the *Annual Survey of Manufacturers* to obtain an estimate of the volume of shipments.

Sources: Census Bureau, *National Trade Databank; Current Industrial Reports* and the *Annual Survey of Manufactures;* Bureau of Labor Statistics; USITC (1989) Pub. No. 2222 (for E_{mm}).

Polyethylene Resins

Under Smoot-Hawley, the tariff rate on low-density polyethylene resins, used in the production of packaging and trash bags, was 4 cents per pound plus 30 percent ad valorem. This rate was successively reduced to 2.75 cents per pound plus 20 percent ad valorem in the Dillon Round, 1.3 cents per pound plus 10 percent ad valorem in the Kennedy Round, and finally to the current rate of 12.5 percent ad valorem in the Tokyo Round.

Effects of eliminating the tariff
(millions of dollars unless noted)

Consumer surplus gain	176
Producer surplus loss	95
Tariff revenue loss	60
Efficiency gain	20
Employment loss (number of workers)	298

Base-year data (1990)		Postliberalization estimates	
Import price (Pm) (dollars/pound)	0.38	Import price (Pm') (dollars/pound)	0.34
Import volume (Qm) (millions of pounds)	1,503	Import volume (Qm') (millions of pounds)	2,501
Domestic price (Pd) (dollars/pound)	0.43	Domestic price (Pd') (dollars/pound)	0.42
Domestic output (Qd) (millions of pounds)	17,875	Domestic output (Qd') (millions of pounds)	17,428
Employment[a] (production workers)	11,900	Employment (production workers)	11,602

PARAMETERS

Elasticities		Constants		Price effect of barrier	
E_{dd}	-0.90	lna	9.35	Average ad valorem tariff (percent)	12.0
E_{dm}	0.33	lnb	11.48		
E_s	2.00	lnc	6.19		
E_{mm}	-5.09				
E_{md}	4.50				
θ	0.1				

a. Assumes that the proportion of all production workers in SIC 2821 (plastic materials and resins) producing polyethylene resins is the same as the share of those resins in the total value of shipments under SIC 2821.

Sources: USITC Office of Industry, personal communication; Bureau of Labor Statistics; USITC (1989) Pub. No. 2222 (for E_{dd} and E_{mm}).

Rubber Footwear (SIC 3021)

In 1933 rubber footwear imports were brought under the American Selling Price (ASP) system of customs valuation, under which the dutiable import value is the wholesale price of a like or competitive domestic product rather than the export price in the country of origin (the usual benchmark). After implementation of the 1963 tariff schedule, 75 percent of rubber footwear imports, by quantity, entered the United States under TSUS item 700.60, dutiable at 20 percent ad valorem and valued on an ASP basis.

In 1980 the ASP system was abolished as a result of concessions in the Tokyo Round. Rubber footwear was divided into nine new categories, initially dutiable at rates ranging from 6 to 67.5 percent ad valorem. Additional Tokyo Round concessions further lowered the rates on some categories of rubber footwear. Ad valorem rates on some protective rubber footwear (e.g., hunting boots, galoshes, and overshoes) dropped from 12.5 percent to 6.6 percent, while other categories remained dutiable at the Smoot-Hawley rates of 25 to 37.5 percent. Ad valorem duties on casual footwear (e.g., athletic footwear, sport oxfords, sneakers, and espadrilles) currently range from 20 to 67 percent, while tariffs on zoris (inexpensive rubber-thonged sandals) have fallen to 2.4 percent ad valorem. Zoris are also the only category of rubber footwear eligible for reduced tariff treatment under the Generalized System of Preferences.

Effects of eliminating the tariff
(millions of dollars unless noted)

Consumer surplus gain	208
Producer surplus loss	55
Tariff revenue loss	141
Efficiency gain	12
Employment loss (number of workers)	1,701

Base-year data (1990)		Postliberalization estimates	
Import price (Pm) (dollars/pair)	4.24	Import price (Pm′) (dollars/pair)	3.53
Import volume (Qm) (millions of pairs)	199	Import volume (Qm′) (millions of pairs)	232
Domestic price (Pd) (dollars/pair)	6.46	Domestic price (Pd′) (dollars/pair)	5.80
Domestic output (Qd) (millions of pairs)	92	Domestic output (Qd′) (millions of pairs)	74
Employment (production workers)	8,800	Employment (production workers)	7,099

PARAMETERS

Elasticities		Constants		Price effect of barrier	
E_{dd}	−2.83	lna	5.71	Average ad valorem	20
E_{dm}	2.83	lnb	0.79	tariff (percent)[a]	
E_s	2.00	lnc	4.45		
E_{mm}	−2.00				
E_{md}	2.00				
θ	0.6				

a. The average ad valorem equivalent tariff, as calculated from the value of collected duties, dropped from 41 percent in 1985–88 to 23 percent in 1989 and 20 percent in 1990, apparently because of the reclassification of items resulting from the conversion to the Harmonized Tariff System.

Sources: Footwear Industries of America (1991); Census Bureau, *Current Industrial Reports;* Bureau of Labor Statistics; USITC (1989) Pub. No. 2222 (for E_{mm}).

Softwood Lumber

In 1986, under the threat of a countervailing duty investigation in the United States, Canada agreed in a memorandum of understanding (MOU) to impose a 15 percent export tax on certain softwood lumber products. About 95 percent of lumber imports come from Canada, of which 90 percent are softwood lumber. Canadian softwood lumber accounted for 33 percent of domestic consumption in 1985 but declined gradually to about 27 percent in 1990. In 1991 Canada claimed the alleged subsidies had been eliminated (only 5 percent of Canadian softwood lumber exports to the United States were still covered under the MOU), withdrew from the MOU as provided for in the agreement, and stopped collecting the export charges. In response, the US Trade Representative initiated a countervailing duty investigation, and in the interim began collecting temporary duties of up to 15 percent ad valorem on imports of softwood lumber products from certain parts of Canada (approximately 20 percent of total imports of Canadian lumber).

In their final determinations in June 1992, the US International Trade Commission and Commerce found "reasonable indication" of injury or threat of injury to the US industry from Canadian subsidies, and a 6.51 percent countervailing duty (CVD) was imposed. Canada challenged the decision before a binational dispute panel under the rules of the Canada-US Free Trade Agreement. The analysis here calculates the welfare impact of the CVD on the US economy; it does not reflect the possible welfare benefits from eliminating distortions in the two economies.

Effects of eliminating the countervailing duty
(millions of dollars unless noted)

Consumer surplus gain	459
Producer surplus loss	264
Duty revenue loss	183
Efficiency gain	12
Employment loss (number of workers)	605

Base-year data (1990)		Postliberalization estimates	
Import price (Pm) (dollars/board foot)	0.239	Import price (Pm') (dollars/board foot)	0.224
Import volume (Qm) (million board feet)	12,182	Import volume (Qm') (million board feet)	13,801
Domestic price (Pd) (dollars/board foot)	0.242	Domestic price (Pd') (dollars/board foot)	0.235
Domestic output (Qd) (millions of board feet)	35,790	Domestic output (Qd') (millions of board feet)	35,435
Employment[a] (production workers)	61,066	Employment (production workers)	60,461

PARAMETERS

Elasticities[b]		Constants		Price effects of barrier	
E_{dd}	−1.45	lna	9.64	Average ad valorem tariff (percent)	0
E_{dm}	0.85	lnb	10.94		
E_s	0.32	lnc	8.52		
E_{mm}	−3.15			Tariff equivalent of CVD (percent)	6.5
E_{md}	2.55				
θ	0.5				

a. Based on the USITC survey finding that producers for half of US production of softwood lumber production employed 30,533 production and related workers in 1990 (USITC Pub. No. 2530, A-39).

b. The value for E_s is from Richardson and Mutti; other parameters are estimated from USITC estimates of the elasticity of aggregate demand (0.3 to 0.6) and the elasticity of substitution between the imported and domestic product (3 to 5) (USITC Pub. No. 2530, 42-43).

Sources: USITC (1992) Pub. No. 2530; Richardson and Mutti 1976 (for E_s).

Women's Footwear, Other than Athletic

SIC 3144 includes women's dress and work shoes, boots, sandals, clogs, and other casual footwear. Women's footwear in this category is made primarily of leather or vinyl and is usually referred to as nonrubber footwear. As a result of the Kennedy Round, tariffs on women's leather and vinyl footwear were approximately cut in half from the Smoot-Hawley rates. From 1968 to 1972, duties on leather footwear were reduced from 18 to 10 percent in staged reductions, and on vinyl footwear from 12.5 to 6 percent.

Currently, women's leather footwear, which accounts for most of the imports under SIC category 3144, is imported under item 700.45 of the TSUS with a duty of 10 percent. Other TSUS items, which have smaller amounts of imports, are subject to duties ranging from 12.5 to 16 percent. Items under TSUS 700.45 are not eligible under either the Generalized System of Preferences or the Caribbean Basin Economic Recovery Act, and they were excluded from the US-Israel free trade area agreement. Nor were tariffs on TSUS 700.45 reduced during the Tokyo Round negotiations.

Effects of eliminating the tariff
(millions of dollars unless noted)

Consumer surplus gain	376
Producer surplus loss	70
Tariff revenue loss	295
Efficiency gain	11
Employment loss (number of workers)	3,702

Base-year data (1990)		Postliberalization estimates	
Import price[a] (Pm) (dollars/pair)	11.89	Import price (Pm') (dollars/pair)	10.81
Import volume[a] (Qm) (millions of pairs)	273	Import volume (Qm') (millions of pairs)	293
Domestic price (Pd) (dollars/pair)	19.78	Domestic price (Pd') (dollars/pair)	18.65
Domestic output (Qd) (millions of pairs)	67	Domestic output (Qd') (millions of pairs)	56
Employment (production workers)	22,800	Employment (production workers)	19,098

PARAMETERS

Elasticities		Constants		Price effect of barrier	
E_{dd}	−4.90	lna	6.70	Average ad valorem tariff (percent)	10.0
E_{dm}	4.90	lnb	−4.75		
E_s	3.00	lnc	4.59		
E_{mm}	−2.00				
E_{md}	2.00				
θ	0.6				

a. Imports of nonrubber footwear have not been broken down by type since the conversion to the Harmonized Tariff System in 1989. These figures were estimated by assuming that the 1989–90 ratio of imports of women's footwear other than athletic (SIC 3144) to imports in the broader category of women's nonrubber footwear, which includes plastic footwear, was the same as for 1985–88.

Sources: Footwear Industries of America (1991); Census Bureau, *Current Industrial Reports;* Bureau of Labor Statistics; USITC (1989) Pub. No. 2222 (for E_{mm}).

Women's Handbags and Purses (SIC 3171)

Smoot-Hawley tariffs on handbags and purses were 35 percent for most leather handbags, 40 to 65 percent for most textile handbags, and 45 percent for most plastic handbags. Prior to the implementation of a new tariff schedule (TSUS) in 1963, only leather handbags were specifically enumerated in the US tariff provisions. Imported handbags of other materials entered under a large number of basket provisions depending largely on the material from which they were made.

The Kennedy Round reduced the rates on handbags (which had been reduced from Smoot-Hawley rates in earlier GATT rounds) to 8.5 percent for reptile leather and 10 percent for other leather. In the Tokyo Round, the rate on handbags of reptile leather was reduced to 5.3 percent. The rate on handbags of other leather valued at more than $20 each was reduced to 9 percent, and the rate on other leather handbags valued at less than $20 was not changed. The rates of duty for handbags of most other materials were reduced to between 6.5 and 21 percent in the Kennedy Round, while the rate of duty for most handbags of plastic remained unchanged at 20 percent. The rates of duty on handbags of beads and of paper yarns were also not reduced and remained at 20 percent and 17.5 percent, respectively.

During the Tokyo Round, concessions were not offered on most handbags made from textiles or plastic because of their import sensitivity. Also, most of these items were excluded from the Generalized System of Preferences and the Caribbean Basin Initiative. In 1984 bilateral quotas under the Multi-Fiber Arrangement were applied to important US suppliers of certain textile handbags.[1]

---

1. For purposes of this case, it is assumed that the quotas are not binding and that only the tariffs restrict imports of women's handbags and purses.

Effects of eliminating the tariff
(millions of dollars unless noted)

Consumer surplus gain	148
Producer surplus loss	16
Tariff revenue loss	119
Efficiency gain	13
Employment loss (number of workers)	773

Base-year data (1990)		Postliberalization estimates	
Import price (Pm) (dollars/unit)	6.15	Import price (Pm') (dollars/unit)	5.42
Import volume (Qm) (millions of units)	163	Import volume (Qm') (millions of units)	199
Domestic price[a] (Pd) (dollars/unit)	16.19	Domestic price (Pd') (dollars/unit)	15.59
Domestic output[a] (Qd) (millions of units)	28	Domestic output (Qd') (millions of units)	26
Employment (production workers)	10,600	Employment (production workers)	9,827

PARAMETERS

Elasticities		Constants		Price effect of barrier	
E_{dd}	-4.44	lna	12.19	Average ad valorem tariff (percent)	13.5
E_{dm}	1.93	lnb	-2.24		
E_s	2.00	lnc	4.85		
E_{mm}	-2.01				
E_{md}	1.40				
θ	0.3				

a. Because volume figures are not consistently available, this figure was derived by calculating a unit value from the 1987 Census of Manufactures and adjusting it upward by the average annual change in the producer price index for handbags for 1988–90. Qd was then calculated by dividing the 1990 value of shipments by this price.

Sources: Census Bureau, National Trade Databank; Annual Survey of Manufactures and Census of Manufactures; Bureau of Labor Statistics; USITC (1989) Pub. No. 2222 (for E_{mm}).

Dairy Products

Regulation of US dairy imports dates back to the Agricultural Adjustment Act of 1933 (see Hufbauer, Berliner, and Elliott 1986). Section 22 of the act authorizes the president to impose duties or quotas on dairy imports if they threaten to harm the domestic industry or government support programs. The dairy price support program was established under the Agricultural Act of 1949. Under this program, the government buys farmers' dairy products when the market price falls below the support price, as established by the secretary of agriculture. Import quotas are needed to maintain the domestic support price. For 1993, the US import quota for cheese—the primary product affected—has been set at 244.2 million pounds. In addition, the United States imposes duties on cheeses, which between 1984 and 1991 averaged approximately 9 percent. As a result of US dairy policy, imports are limited to approximately 2 percent of domestic production.

Calculation of Tariff Equivalents and Elasticities

Since cheese accounts for more than 90 percent of US imports of dairy products, the tariff equivalent is estimated as the difference between the domestic US price of cheese and the landed price of imported cheese (including transportation and other charges and the regular tariff). The elasticities are estimated from the USITC's estimates of $-.33$ for the elasticity of aggregate demand and -1.7 for the elasticity of substitution between the imported and domestically produced good (USITC Pub. No. 2314, app. E).

Because import licenses are allocated to US citizens, it is assumed in this case that US quota holders capture the rents and that there is no quota rent transfer to foreigners. There is some recent empirical evidence, however, to suggest that the export side of the cheese market is sufficiently concentrated that exporters do capture a portion of the rents from the cheese quotas. Flynn and Reinert (1992, 10) assume that the quota rents on cheese are split 50–50 between exporters and importers. That suggests that the net national welfare gain (efficiency gains plus any quota rents recaptured from foreign exporters) in this case may be twice as large as the $104 million efficiency gain estimated here.

Effects of eliminating the quotas
(millions of dollars unless noted)

Consumer surplus gain	1,184
Producer surplus loss	835
Quota rent loss	244
Efficiency gain	104
Employment loss (number of workers)	2,378

Base-year data (average 1989-91)		Postliberalization estimates	
Import price (Pm) (dollars/pound)	2.39	Import price (Pm') (dollars/pound)	1.59
Import volume (Qm) (million pounds)	3.07	Import volume (Qm') (million pounds)	569
Domestic price (Pd) (dollars/pound)	2.55	Domestic price (Pd') (dollars/pound)	2.45
Domestic output (Qd) (million pounds)	8,103	Domestic output (Qd') (million pounds)	7,902
Employment (processing) (production workers)	96,000	Employment (production workers)	93,622

PARAMETERS

Elasticities		Constants		Price effects of barrier	
E_{dd}	-0.37	lna	9.26	Average ad valorem tariff (percent)	8.0
E_{dm}	0.10	lnb	8.44		
E_s	0.60	lnc	5.92		
E_{mm}	-1.66			Tariff equivalent of the quota (percent)	50.0[a]
E_{md}	1.34				
θ	.1				

a. Only the effects of eliminating the quotas are summarized here; it is assumed that the tariff is retained.

Sources: Agricultural Statistics, USDA Economic Research Service; Bureau of Labor Statistics, *Industrial Outlook; Employment and Earnings;* USITC 2314 and 2276 for elasticities; FTC (1990).

Peanuts

The Agricultural Adjustment Act of 1938, as amended in 1941, established market quotas and a price support system based on "parity" for peanuts. In order to prevent imports from undermining the price support program, a strict import quota was established, as provided under section 22 of the Agricultural Adjustment Act of 1933 (as amended in 1935). Since 1953, the annual import quota has remained at 1.71 million pounds (shelled basis).[1]

The quota has been temporarily relaxed in times of drought—in 1954, 1981, and most recently, in 1990, when President Bush temporarily raised the import quota to 100 million pounds (shelled basis). Actual imports reached only 23.1 million pounds (shelled basis)[2] during the crop year ending 1991. Nevertheless, because 1990 was an unusual year, it is excluded from the base-year data used in the calculations.

Calculation of Tariff Equivalent and Elasticities

The tariff equivalent used in this case is an average of the USITC estimates for shelled and unshelled peanuts for crop years 1987–88 and 1988–89 (USITC 2369, 4-34). E_{dd} is calculated from the USITC estimate of -0.7 for the elasticity of aggregate demand and an elasticity of substitution between the domestic and imported products of -4. The absolute value of 13 for the own-price and cross-price elasticities of import demand was selected because it is the lowest value that does not produce a reduction in overall consumption following liberalization.

---

1. Two million pounds on unshelled, farmers' stock basis.

2. 27 million pounds on unshelled basis.

Effects of eliminating the quota
(millions of dollars unless noted)

Consumer surplus gain	54
Producer surplus loss	32
Quota rent gain	negl.
Efficiency gain	22
Employment loss (number of workers)	397

Base-year data (avg 1987/88–88/89)		Postliberalization estimates	
Import price (Pm) (dollars/pound)	0.51	Import price (Pm') (dollars/pound)	0.34
Import volume (Qm) (millions of pounds)	2	Import volume (Qm') (millions of pounds)	258
Domestic price (Pd) (dollars/pound)	0.27	Domestic price (Pd') (dollars/pound)	0.26
Domestic output (Qd) (millions of pounds)	3,800	Domestic output (Qd') (millions of pounds)	3,734
Employment[a] (farm workers)	23,000	Employment (farm workers)	22,603

PARAMETERS

Elasticities		Constants		Price effects of barrier	
E_{dd}	−0.73	lna	7.35	Average ad valorem tariff (percent)	[b]
E_{dm}	0.10	lnb	8.96		
E_s	0.55	lnc	8.96		
E_{mm}	−13.00			Tariff equivalent of the quota (percent)	50
E_{md}	13.00				
θ	0.1				

a. Estimated as the share of peanuts in total gross farm receipts multiplied by total farm employment.

b. The way in which the tariff equivalent was estimated also incorporates any price effect of import duties that may be charged on peanuts (USITC Pub. No. 2276, chapter 4).

Sources: Census Bureau, Statistical Abstract 1991; USITC (1991) Pub. 2369 and (1990a) 2314 (for E_{dt} and E_s).

Sugar

Import quotas on sugar, which had been in effect for most of the period since 1934, were effectively allowed to lapse in 1974 during a period of booming prices and domestic inflation. Quotas were reimposed in 1982 and regularly tightened throughout the mid-1980s as world prices collapsed (Hufbauer, Berliner, and Elliott 1986). Although a statutory tariff is also imposed on a most-favored nation (MFN) basis, most US sugar is imported from countries benefiting from duty-free status under either the Caribbean Basin Initiative or the Generalized System of Preferences so that the value of duties actually collected is negligible.

In 1989, Australia, whose share of the US sugar quota had dropped from 232,000 short tons in 1982 to 58,000 short tons in 1988, brought a formal complaint against the US sugar quota system under the General Agreement on Tariffs and Trade (GATT). A GATT dispute settlement panel ruled that the US quota system was in violation of GATT rules since the rules allow import quotas only as part of an agricultural policy that also controls domestic production. Australia argued successfully that under the US system, imports had borne a disproportionate share of declining US demand (Barry 1991, 8).

The United States therefore replaced this quota with a tariff-rate quota (TRQ), which nominally allows imports to respond to increasing demand. Whereas a quota imposes an absolute limit on the amount that can be imported, a TRQ allows imports above the quota ceiling as long as imports pay an additional duty. But in practice, the system remains relatively rigid because the over-quota duty was set at a prohibitive level (16 cents per pound). In an attempt to mollify foreign exporters, however, the 1990 Farm Act also required the secretary of agriculture to impose controls on domestic production if the projected difference between domestic sugar supply and demand is less than 1.25 million short tons, effectively providing a floor of that amount for imports (Barry 1991, 8–9).

US quotas on sugar

Year	Millions of pounds
December 1985–December 1986	3,784.0
January 1987–December 1987	2,232.6
January 1988–December 1988	1,650.0
January 1989–September 1990	4,971.7
October 1990–September 1991	3,795.0
October 1991–September 1992	3,047.0

Calculation of Tariff Equivalent and Elasticities

The price effect of the quotas in this case is estimated as the difference between the price of imports in the US market, inclusive of quota rents, and the low-cost foreign producer price plus 1.5 cents per pound for handling charges (*International Financial Statistics;* FTC 1990, 31; USITC 1990, 2–4). The price elasticities of demand are calculated from a variety of estimates indicating that the elasticity of aggregate demand is -0.1 or less and that the elasticity of substitution is about 5 (Australian Bureau of Agricultural and Resource Economics 1990; Federal Trade Commission 1990; Maskus 1989; Tarr and Morkre 1984; Tyers and Anderson 1989; and US International Trade Commission 1990, appendix E).

Effects of eliminating the TRQ
(millions of dollars unless noted)

Consumer surplus gain	1,357
Producer surplus loss	776
Quota rent gain	396
Efficiency gain	185
Employment loss (number of workers)	2,261

Base-year data (1990)		Postliberalization estimates	
Import price (Pm) (dollars/short ton)	466	Import price (Pm') (dollars/short ton)	280
Import volume (Qm) (thousands of short tons)	2,129	Import volume (Qm') (thousands of short tons)	4,117
Domestic price (Pd) (dollars/short ton)	466	Domestic price (Pd') (dollars/short ton)	331
Domestic output (Qd) (thousands of short tons)	6,319	Domestic output (Qd') (thousands of short tons)	5,143
Employment[a] (processing) (production workers)	12,150	Employment (production workers)	9,889

PARAMETERS

Elasticities		Constants		Price effects of barrier	
E_{dd}	−1.33	lna	8.94	Average ad valorem tariff (percent)	0[b]
E_{dm}	1.30	lnb	5.06		
E_s	0.60	lnc	8.22		
E_{mm}	−3.78			Tariff equivalent of quota (percent)	66
E_{md}	3.69				
θ	0.7				

a. Excludes estimated number of workers in cane refining, who could more easily switch to imported inputs than cane or sugar beet mills.

b. Although there is a statutory duty on imported sugar of 0.625 cents/pound, the majority of sugar is imported from countries eligible for benefits under either the Caribbean Basin Initiative or the Generalized System of Preferences, so that actual duties collected are negligible.

Sources: USDA 1990, 8 and 35; 1991, 56; USITC (1990), Pub. No. 2314 appendix E for elasticities.

Maritime Services Involving Cabotage

The US maritime industry has received government support and protection from foreign competition since the founding of the republic. A higher per ton tax rate was imposed on foreign ships entering US ports than on American ships in the Tariff Act of 1789; later the same act provided for a 10 percent rebate on customs duties for goods carried by US ships; the first cabotage law, governing trade between US ports, was passed in 1817. In addition to favorable tax rates and cabotage laws, the US government has also reserved certain government cargoes for US-flag shipping (cargo preference laws) and has provided direct subsidies to both shipbuilders and shipping companies (Hufbauer, Berliner, and Elliott 1986).

Since the early 1980s, support for the US maritime industries has declined sharply. The Reagan administration in the mid-1980s eliminated shipbuilding subsidies and significantly reduced subsidies to offset the higher cost of operating US-flag ships (which must be American-built and American-staffed to be eligible). The major remaining trade barrier in maritime services is the Jones Act of 1920, the cabotage law currently in effect which requires that trade between US ports be shipped in US-flag ships, built in the United States and crewed by Americans.

Methodological Notes

The Jones Act affects shipping on inland waterways and the Great Lakes as well as shipping along and between the US coasts. Because the Jones Act completely bans the carriage of freight on foreign ships between US ports, there are no directly comparable imports to serve as a base for the calculations in the model. However, there is some traffic on US inland waterways that is of foreign origin, mostly ships traveling between US and Canadian ports (personal communication, Frank Smith, ENO Foundation for Transportation). Some data are available on the magnitude of this trade, and this serves as the import base on which the effects of liberalization are modeled. In essence, we treat this case as a tariff-rate quota on the market for shipping services along and between the American coasts and on US inland waterways. The tariff is zero for trade in these waters that is not subject to the Jones Act, i.e., trade that begins on a US inland waterway and continues on to a foreign port such as Montreal.[1]

---

1. Since the "under-quota" tariff in this case is zero, no quota rents are created in this case.

The "over-quota" tariff on trade subject to the Jones Act is then derived from the model, starting with a calculation of the increase in imports resulting from liberalization, which is derived as follows. Foreign-owned shipping companies already involved in foreign trade to and from the United States seem the most likely to be competitive in trade along and between the US Atlantic and Pacific coasts. Nearly 90 percent of the coastwise trade (measured in ton-miles) represents transport of crude petroleum and petroleum products. Since many of those tankers are owned by the oil companies themselves and represent sunk costs, repeal of the Jones Act would probably have little effect in the short run. According to a recent US International Trade Commission report (USITC Pub. No. 2495), however, half the US Jones Act tanker fleet (which accounts for two-thirds of the Jones Act ocean-going fleet) is at least 23 years old, and two-thirds is at least 17 years old. Since the "useful economic life" of a ship is usually 25 to 30 years, it seems likely that if the Jones Act were repealed in 1994, within five years or so many of the current US-flag tankers would be replaced with foreign-flag ships. It would probably be more difficult, however, for foreign shippers to penetrate shipping on inland waterways.

It is assumed here that, in the long run, foreign shippers would capture 50 percent of the coastwise Jones Act trade if the act were repealed, somewhat below the share they currently hold of US foreign trade. In addition, it is assumed more conservatively that foreign shippers would capture only 25 percent of inland waterway trade on rivers, canals, and the Great Lakes.

Effects of repealing the Jones Act
(millions of dollars unless noted)

Consumer surplus gain	1,832
Producer surplus loss	1,275
Quota rent gain[a]	0
Efficiency gain	556
Employment loss (number of workers)	4,411

Base-year data (1990)		Postliberalization estimates	
Import price[b] (Pm) (index)	1.00	Import price (Pm') (index)	0.54
Import volume[a] (Qm) (millions of dollars)	1,227	Import volume (Qm') (millions of dollars)	3,627
Domestic price (Pd) (index)	1.00	Domestic price (Pd') (index)	0.78
Domestic output[c] (Qd) (millions of dollars)	6,500	Domestic output (Qd') (millions of dollars)	5,066
Employment (number of workers)	20,000	Employment (number of workers)	15,589

PARAMETERS

Elasticities[d]		Constants		Price effects of barrier	
E_{dd}	−2.40	lna	8.78	Average ad valorem tariff (percent)	0.00
E_{dm}	1.36	lnb	8.78		
E_s	1.00	lnc	7.11		
E_{mm}	−2.90			Tariff equivalent (percent)	85.0
E_{md}	2.90				
θ	0.4				

a. Because the Jones Act bans imports entirely, there are no quota rents; see methodological notes for the method of calculating a proxy figure for the import volume of similar shipping services.

b. Since this category encompasses many services, data on the aggregate volume of products are not available. Instead, the value of shipments and imports must be used in place of the volumes, and an index is used for the prices.

c. Assumes the proportion of the nation's freight bill attributable to foreign ships passing through inland waterways is the same as the share when measured in ton-miles.

d. Calculations based on USITC estimates of a price elasticity of total demand of −3.5 to −5.5, and a fairly high elasticity of substitution of −3 (USITC Pub. No. 2422).

Sources: Eno Transportation Foundation (1992); Bureau of Labor Statistics, *Employment and Earnings;* USITC (1990b) Pub. No. 2422 for elasticities.

Textiles and Apparel

The textile and apparel industries in the United States have enjoyed increasing protection from imports throughout the postwar period. Beginning in 1957, when voluntary restraint agreements were negotiated with Japan, coverage has continued to expand, encompassing a greater number of materials and suppliers. Trade in the textile and apparel industries is now managed under the fourth Multi-Fiber Arrangement (MFA IV).[1] MFA IV was implemented on 31 July 1986 with a planned duration of five years. It was supposed to be replaced with a new regime, negotiated in the Uruguay Round of multilateral trade negotiations under the General Agreement on Tariffs and Trade (GATT). When the Uruguay Round failed to conclude as scheduled at the end of 1990, MFA IV was renewed—with no substantive revisions—in July 1991 and again in December 1992. The current extension expires on 31 December 1993.

In negotiating MFA IV, the United States and other highly developed nations sought to expand the restrictions of MFA III, primarily by extending coverage to previously unrestricted materials, by freezing or rolling back imports from major suppliers, and through increased protection from "import surges." As a result, the number of restricted materials was expanded to include linen, ramie, silk, vegetable fibers, or blends thereof. Protection from import surges was accommodated by permitting the elimination of consistently underused quotas and by allowing nations to negotiate resolutions through bilateral agreements. Finally, in dealing with major suppliers, MFA IV allows for "new restraints that are mutually accepted," which in practice has resulted in the curtailment of quota growth and even rollbacks in import volumes (GATT, "Extension of the Multifibre Arrangement Agreed," press release, GATT/1390, Geneva, 5 August 1986).

The agreement did stipulate that small or new suppliers be given preferential treatment and that cotton textiles from cotton-producing nations be given special consideration in terms of market liberalization, but in terms of market liberalization overall, MFA IV was a step backward from previous arrangements. As noted by William R. Cline, "The tone of the renewal is one of ample scope for restricting imports at will, especially those from major suppliers. The original MFA target of 6 percent growth in import levels appears all but abandoned" (Cline 1990, 220).

The MFA reforms under negotiation in the Uruguay Round call for a gradual phase-out of quotas in favor of tariffs, which would then be reduced according to regular GATT rules. The draft serving as the basis for negotiations as of spring 1993 (the so-called Dunkel draft) called for textile and apparel trade to be brought back under the auspices of GATT rules within

---

1. For more on the history of protection in the United States through MFA III, see Hufbauer, Berliner, and Elliott (1986).

10 years. The administration of President Bill Clinton, under pressure from the domestic industries, however, has raised the possibility of extending the adjustment period to 15 years. The European textile and apparel industries are also seeking a 15-year adjustment period. In addition, the US and European industries are seeking to maintain a "cliff" of protection up to the end of the adjustment period (in hopes that protection will then be extended for a further period). The Dunkel draft, by contrast, calls for degressive protection with pro rata liberalization year by year.

Methodological Notes

An index system had to be used to represent import and domestic product prices because volume data for domestic production are not available. The average tariff is calculated from data on the value of imports (by SIC categories) and duties collected, published in Department of Commerce publication FT 990. Because of problems associated with the conversion to the Harmonized Tariff System (HTS), comparable data were not published after 1988, so the average tariffs used in these cases are based on the average tariff in 1984 to 1988. The (weighted) average tariff equivalents are calculated from data on 1987 tariff equivalents, by category, reported in USITC Pub. No. 2222. Cline's calculations for the other parameters are adopted here.

The estimates derived from the USITC data are similar to those used by Cline (1990, chapter 6), who surveyed the literature and concluded that tariff equivalents of 30.5 percent for apparel and 16 percent for textiles were reasonable for the period after 1986, when bilateral quotas for major suppliers and the MFA were tightened. Although the USITC and Cline tariff equivalents are for 1987 and 1986, respectively, import data indicate little if any liberalization of textile and apparel trade since then. For both textiles and apparel, import growth rates slowed markedly in the late 1980s. The market share of textile imports has barely changed since 1987 (on a customs value basis); it was 8.8 percent in 1991 and 8.6 percent in 1987. The import market share for apparel grew more, from 23 percent in 1987 to almost 27 percent in 1991 (again on a customs value basis), but the average unit value of apparel imports increased more than 10 percent over the same period, indicating that some of the increase may have been due to quality upgrading, rather than liberalization.[2]

Finally, it should be noted that the net national welfare gain from recapturing quota rents from foreign exporters may be overstated. Recent empirical research suggests that in some cases importing firms may be large enough to capture a portion of the rents for themselves (see Goto 1989, 218; Erzan, Krishna, and Tan 1991; Reinert 1993).

---

2. Data on the volume of domestic production are not available, so import penetration ratios can only be calculated on a value basis.

Effects of liberalizing the MFA for textiles
(millions of dollars unless noted)

Consumer surplus gain	3,274
Producer surplus loss	1,749
Tariff revenue loss	632
Quota rent gain	713
Efficiency gain	181
Employment loss (number of workers)	16,203

Base-year data (1990)		Postliberalization estimates	
Import price (Pm) (index)	1.00	Import price (Pm') (index)	0.81
Import volume (Qm) (millions of dollars)	7,079	Import volume (Qm') (millions of dollars)	8,981
Domestic price (Pd) (index)	1.00	Domestic price (Pd') (index)	0.97
Domestic output (Qd) (millions of dollars)	64,986	Domestic output (Qd') (millions of dollars)	63,213
Employment (production workers)	594,000	Employment (production workers)	577,797

PARAMETERS

Elasticities		Constants		Price effects of barrier	
E_{dd}	−0.60	lna	11.08	Average ad valorem tariff (percent)	11.0
E_{dm}	0.21	lnb	11.08		
E_s	1.00	lnc	8.86		
E_{mm}	−1.30			Tariff equivalent of VRAs (percent)	12.4
E_{md}	1.30				
θ	.13			Total tariff equivalent assumed eliminated (percent)	23.4

Effects of liberalizing the MFA for apparel
(millions of dollars unless noted)

Consumer surplus gain	21,158
Producer surplus loss	9,901
Tariff revenue loss	3,545
Quota rent gain	5,411
Efficiency gain	2,301
Employment loss (number of workers)	152,583

Base-year data (1990)		Postliberalization estimates	
Import price (Pm) (index)	1.00	Import price (Pm') (index)	0.68
Import volume (Qm) (millions of dollars)	27,641	Import volume (Qm') (millions of dollars)	41,847
Domestic price (Pd) (index)	1.00	Domestic price (Pd') (index)	0.82
Domestic output (Qd) (millions of dollars)	61,962	Domestic output (Qd') (millions of dollars)	51,111
Employment (production workers)	871,300	Employment (production workers)	718,717

PARAMETERS

Elasticities		Constants		Price effects of barrier	
E_{dd}	−1.40	lna	11.03	Average ad valorem tariff (percent)	19.0
E_{dm}	1.18	lnb	11.03		
E_s	1.00	lnc	10.23		
E_{mm}	−1.60			Tariff equivalent of VRAs (percent)	29.0
E_{md}	1.10				
θ	.5			Total tariff equivalent assumed eliminated (percent)	48.0

Sources (both tables): Department of Commerce, Office of Textiles and Apparel, *Major Shipper Report;* International Trade Administration, *Industrial Outlook*; Bureau of Labor Statistics; Cline (1990, 365); Census Bureau, FT 990; USITC (1989) Pub. No. 2222 for elasticities.

Machine Tools

On 20 May 1986, acting under section 232 of the Trade Expansion Act of 1962, which authorizes the imposition of import restrictions for reasons of national security, President Ronald Reagan announced that he would seek "voluntary" export restraint agreements (VRAs) with major suppliers of certain machine tools. Import relief was granted for 7 of the 18 categories of machine tools that were the subject of the section 232 investigation—horizontal numerically controlled (NC) lathes, vertical NC lathes, non-NC lathes, milling machines, machining centers, and NC and non-NC punching and shearing machines. These categories accounted for approximately one-half of all US machine tool imports (White House Fact Sheet, 20 May 1986). President Reagan also announced a Domestic Action Plan to revitalize the US machine tool industry. On 16 December 1986 the administration announced that it had signed VRAs with Japan and Taiwan restricting their exports for the period 1 January 1987 to 31 December 1991. Two other major suppliers— Germany and Switzerland—refused to submit to formal arrangements.[1] Both agreed to informal limitations on their exports of certain machine tool categories, however.

Japan agreed to restrict exports in three categories (NC lathes, machining centers, and NC punching and shearing machines) to their 1981 market share levels—reductions of from 9 to 24 percent—and agreed not to exceed their 1985 market shares in the other three categories.[2] Taiwan agreed to reduce exports of milling machines and non-NC lathes to their 1981 market share, a reduction of about 30 percent, and agreed not to exceed their 1985 market shares for NC lathes and machining centers. To prevent shifts into higher-valued product lines, Japan and Taiwan also agreed to maintain their 1985 product mixes in the restricted machine tool categories.

Informally, Germany agreed not to exceed its 1981 market share for non-NC punching and shearing machines, or its 1985 market share for machining centers, NC and non-NC lathes, and NC punching and shearing machines. Switzerland also agreed to limit its exports of NC punching and shearing machines to the 1985 market share level. In addition to these arrangements, seven other countries were sent presidential letters

---

1. Under the Treaty of Rome, Germany is prohibited from concluding bilateral trade agreements. Switzerland has a firm national policy of avoiding bilateral trade agreements and also claims that it has no legal means to enforce them (Hooley 1987, 18).

2. Limitations on NC lathes, machining centers, and NC punching and shearing machines were to be controlled through export licenses. Limitations on the other categories were to be controlled through administrative guidance; no export licenses for these products would be required as long as exports did not exceed agreed limits (White House Release, 16 December 1986).

requesting that they not exceed their 1986 import penetration levels.[3] The VRAs with Japan and Taiwan were extended in 1991.

Methodological Notes

Whether for economic or political reasons, US import statistics indicate that foreign suppliers other than Japan, Taiwan, Germany, and Switzerland did not fully offset the reduction in imports from the restrained suppliers:

	Imports from affected suppliers (units)	Imports from unaffected suppliers (units)
1985	17,892	8,380
1986	16,739	8,152
1987	11,318	6,552
1988	11,139	8,982
1989	12,335	8,515
1990	10,102	10,735

Thus, the effect of the VRA program is assumed to be the decline in average 1989–90 total imports from all suppliers by comparison with the 1986 level. To the degree that other factors—exchange rate changes, changes in demand, etc.—account for the decline, this methodology overstates the impact of the import restraint program.

---

3. Brazil, Italy, Korea, Singapore, Sweden, and the United Kingdom were identified as other significant machine tool suppliers and were asked to restrict their exports to the United States (GAO 1990, 8).

Effects of eliminating the voluntary restraint agreements
(millions of dollars unless noted)

Consumer surplus gain	542
Producer surplus loss	157
Quota rent gain	350
Efficiency gain	35
Employment loss (number of workers)	1,534

Base-year data (average 1989-90)		Postliberalization estimates	
Import price (Pm) (dollars/unit)	52,721	Import price (Pm') (dollars/unit)	35,952
Import volume (Qm) (thousands of units)	20.8	Import volume (Qm') (thousands of units)	25.0
Domestic price (Pd) (dollars/unit)	73,304	Domestic price (Pd') (dollars/unit)	62,924
Domestic output (Qd) (thousands of units)	16.3	Domestic output (Qd') (thousands of units)	14.0
Employment (production workers)	10,870	Employment (production workers)	9,336

PARAMETERS

Elasticities		Constants		Price effects of barrier	
E_{dd}	-0.73	lna	3.47	Average ad valorem	4.0
E_{dm}	0.69	lnb	-8.41	tariff (percent)	
E_s	1.00	lnc	2.78		
E_{mm}	-0.79			Tariff equivalent	46.6
E_{md}	0.79			of VRAs[a] (percent)	
θ	.4				

a. Only the welfare effects of eliminating the VRAs are summarized here; it is assumed that the tariff is retained.

Sources: National Machine Tool Builders Association (1990); Census Bureau, *Current Industrial Report;* Reinert and Roland-Holst (1992) (for E_{md}).

Appendix ‖

Cases Not Effective in 1990

Automobiles: Potential Effects of Proposed Protection for the Industry

Early in 1992, the Japanese government announced that it would reduce the ceiling for auto exports under its "voluntary" restraint arrangement, in place since 1981, from 2.30 million units per year to 1.65 million units per year. Both prior to and following the Japanese announcement, a number of proposals for restricting auto imports from Japan were floated by industry representatives and members of Congress. Among them were proposals for capping total sales of Japanese autos in the United States, including production from the "transplants" (Japanese-owned plants in the United States) and an effort to get the US Customs Service to reclassify minivans and sport utility vehicles (SUVs) as light trucks. Reclassification would have the effect of raising the tariff from 2.5 percent ad valorem to 25 percent ad valorem (the so-called "Chicken War" tariff imposed on small trucks in the wake of a US-EC trade dispute in 1963).

Estimating the effects of the proposals to limit total Japanese market share in the United States requires a number of simplifying assumptions regarding, for example, market growth, market shares of the suppliers, the Japanese response, and price trends. Since changes in any one of these assumptions would change the results, in some cases dramatically, only the potential effects of the reduction in the VRA ceiling and the proposed reclassification of minivans and SUVs are estimated here. The estimated effects of the Japanese VRA may serve as the low end of the range for proposals that would restrict total Japanese market share in the United States. The effect of an overall cap on Japanese market share might be small at first (assuming no initial reduction in market share), but the costs to the US economy would grow over time as Japanese firms bumped against their ceiling. At some point, the costs would surpass those of the VRA on Japanese exports since the Japanese producers would not be able to shift production to their US plants.

Description of the Scenarios

Though the Japanese VRA may have been binding for some companies in the late 1980s, aggregate Japanese auto exports have not reached the 2.3 million-unit level since 1987—primarily because of increased production by the transplants. Scenario 1 assumes that in the absence of political pressure and with the US recession, the Japanese would have exported the same number of automobiles to the United States in 1992 as in 1991.[1] In this scenario, the effects of reducing that level to 1.65

---

1. In fact, Japanese exports did not reach the VRA ceiling of $1.65 million in fiscal 1992 and likely will not at an exchange rate of 105 yen to the dollar (*International Trade Reporter*, 31 March, 1993, 534).

million units are then estimated. The scenario assumes that the Japanese transplants respond only to the induced price changes and do not automatically offset decreased exports with increased production in the United States. Based on the findings of Dinopoulos and Kreinen (1988) with regard to the earlier VRA, it also assumes that the European producers raise their prices rather than increase their market shares.

No adjustment is made for quality upgrading by Japanese or European firms (an adjustment was made by Feenstra and by de Melo and Tarr for the mid-1980s). However, the degree to which the absence of an adjustment overstates the costs of the VRA is tempered by three factors. First, as pointed out by Tarr (1989) and Jones (1989), improved quality reduces choice at the lower end of the market and may lower welfare for consumers who do not value the added options at the price they are charged. Second, given the upgrading Japanese exporters have already done, both in terms of new models and more options on old models, there may be less scope for upgrading now than a decade ago. Finally, Dinopolous and Kreinen (1988), who did make adjustments for quality upgrading, found that European producers raised quality-adjusted prices on their exports more per unit than did the Japanese, suggesting that quality upgrading was less of a factor in price increases for European cars than it was for Japanese cars in the first round of VERs.

Scenario 2 estimates the effects of raising the tariff on minivans and sport utility vehicles from 2.5 percent to 25 percent. Although the impact of the tariff was sufficient earlier in the decade to encourage Nissan to move its production of light trucks to its US plant, no adjustment is made in this scenario for the possibility that Toyota and Mazda would respond to the tariff hike by moving production to their US facilities.

Methodological Notes

Volume and value data on US imports and exports of passenger cars are available in the USITC monthly reports on the auto industry. The volume of shipments by the Big Three US producers (GM, Ford, and Chrysler) and the Japanese transplants is available from *Ward's Automotive Yearbook*, but the values must be estimated. For the Big Three, domestic shipment unit values are assumed the same as US export unit values (from the USITC). For the Japanese transplants, the unit value of imports from Japan is used, expressed on a c.i.f., duty-paid basis. Because of the dominance of the Big Three in Canadian production, imports from Canada are also included as part of domestic US production. Thus, the volume of domestic output (Qd) is the sum of output by the Big Three, the Japanese transplants, and imports from Canada; the domestic price (Pd) is a weighted average of the US and Japanese transplant unit values as described above plus the unit value of Canadian imports. Qm, then, is the quantity of imports from all sources other than Canada, and Pm

is the unit value of those same imports. The figure for employment is for SIC 3711, which includes car bodies as well as assembled motor vehicles. (Because SIC 3711 includes more than just the assembly of passenger cars, it already overstates the employment impact of the proposed restrictions; thus we did not attempt to incorporate Canadian employment data, even though we include Canadian production in domestic output.)

Data on the volume and value of US producers' shipments of minivans and SUVs, and of Japanese exports to the United States of SUVs, are contained in the recent USITC report (Pub. No. 2529) resulting from its investigation of possible injury to the US industry caused by Japanese dumping of minivans. The volume of Japanese exports of minivans is from *Ward's*, while the unit value is assumed the same as for SUVs. Chrysler imports some minivans from its Canada plant and GM some SUVs, so imports from Canada again are treated as domestic production; however, they must be estimated. Since almost all US imports of SUVs are from either Canada or Japan, the volume and value of Canadian exports are estimated as the difference between total imports and imports from Japan (contained in the USITC report). Imports from Canada of minivans are estimated as the difference between sales of "domestic makes" (as classified by *Ward's*, which include Canadian production by the Big Three) and production in the United States as estimated by the USITC. The unit value of imports of minivans from Canada (which serve the low end of the market) is assumed to be the same as for SUV imports from Canada (USITC report).

Estimates of the own-price elasticities of demand for all imported and domestically produced motor vehicles are reported in Tarr (1989). The USITC reports a much higher estimate of the price elasticity of demand for Japanese cars but cites other estimates indicating that the demand has become less elastic over time. An average of the Tarr and USITC import-demand elasticities is used here. The other elasticities are calculated using the relationships sketched in chapter 3. Since the own-price elasticities of demand were estimated before the Japanese transplants were a significant factor, the value of shipments from those plants is excluded from the value of domestic shipments used in estimating the cross-elasticities.

Because separate elasticities of demand for minivans have not been estimated, values from scenario 1 are retained in scenario 2 for the own-price elasticities of demand, and the cross-price elasticities are then calculated from that base. Scenario 2 represents a middle-range estimate of the effects of the tariff increase. If the elasticity of demand for imported minivans and SUVs is higher than assumed, the costs of raising the tariff would be less than shown here. But if the elasticities of demand for both the domestic and imported products are higher than assumed, the costs would be higher than reported here.

Effects of lowering the VRA ceiling
(millions of dollars unless noted)

Consumer surplus loss	1,741
Producer surplus gain	461
Quota rent loss[a]	1,244
Efficiency loss	36
Employment gain[b] (number of workers)	1,234

Base-year data (1991)		Postrestriction estimates	
Import price (Pm) (dollars/unit)	12,700	Import price (Pm') (dollars/unit)	13,218
Import volume (Qm) (millions of units)	2.54	Import volume (Qm') (millions of units)	2.40
Domestic price[c] (Pd) (dollars/unit)	12,600	Domestic price (Pd') (dollars/unit)	12,669
Domestic output[d] (Qd) (millions of units)	6.64	Domestic output (Qd') (millions of units)	6.68
Employment[e] (production workers)	224,700	Employment (production workers)	225,934

PARAMETERS

Elasticities		Constants		Price effects of barrier	
E_{dd}	−1.19	lna	24.11	Average ad valorem tariff (percent)	2.5
E_{dm}	0.30	lnb	6.27		
E_s	1.00	lnc	23.26		
E_{mm}	−1.50			Tariff equivalent of the VRA[f] (percent)	4.1
E_{md}	0.60				
θ	.15				

a. The amount that is transferred to foreigners, hence the national welfare loss, will be less than indicated if the foreign producers allow their dealers to capture a portion of the rents, as the Japanese reportedly did in the 1980s (de Melo and Tarr 1992, 82).

b. Implicitly includes some Canadian jobs since domestic production includes imports from Canada.

c. Assumed the same as for exports.

d. Includes imports from Canada.

e. Employment in US plants only.

f. Only the effects of eliminating the VRA are summarized here.

Effects of increasing the tariff on minivans and SUVs
(millions of dollars unless noted)

Consumer surplus loss	987
Producer surplus gain	222
Tariff revenue gain	655
Efficiency loss	110
Employment gain[a] (number of workers)	203

Base-year data (1991)		Postrestriction estimates	
Import price (Pm) (dollars/unit)	17,700	Import price (Pm') (dollars/unit)	21,680
Import volume (Qm) (millions of units)	.220	Import volume (Qm') (millions of units)	.165
Domestic price (Pd) (dollars/unit)	15,200	Domestic price (Pd') (dollars/unit)	15,341
Domestic output[b] (Qd) (millions of units)	1.560	Domestic output (Qd') (millions of units)	1.575
Employment[c] (production workers)	21,862	Employment (production workers)	22,065

PARAMETERS

Elasticities		Constants		Price effects of barrier	
E_{dd}	−1.19	lna	24.74	Ad valorem	2.5
E_{dm}	0.10	lnb	4.63	tariff (percent)	
E_{s}	1.00	lnc	12.53		
E_{mm}	−1.50			Proposed increase	22.5
E_{md}	1.50			in the ad valorem	
θ	.05			tariff[d] (percent)	

a. Implicitly includes some Canadian jobs since domestic production includes imports from Canada.

b. Includes imports from Canada.

c. Employment in US plants only.

d. The welfare effects summarized here result from the proposed increase in the tariff rate; welfare effects of the regular 2.5 percent tariff are not included.

Sources: See text.

Flat-Rolled Steel Products

In the heat of the 1988 election campaign, then–presidential candidate George Bush promised Pennsylvania Senator John Heinz that, if elected, Bush would seek an international agreement to eliminate unfair trade practices in steel and in the interim would extend the "voluntary" restraint agreements (VRAs), negotiated in 1985, when they expired in September 1989 (see Hufbauer, Berliner, and Elliott 1986 for the history of steel protection). Although the steel industry sought another five years of restraints, the Bush administration granted an extension only through March 1992 and also provided as much as an additional percentage point increase annually in the total import market share to be allotted to countries entering into "bilateral consensus agreements" to reduce subsidies and other steel trade barriers (USITC Pub. No. 2248).

The VRAs were allowed to expire as planned at the end of March 1992. Three months later, several US steel producers filed a number of petitions alleging that steel producers in 20 countries were illegally subsidized or were dumping their products in the US market. In August, the US International Trade Commission preliminarily determined that there was a "reasonable indication" that US producers had been injured in 72 of the 84 cases filed. The International Trade Administration of the US Department of Commerce released its findings of preliminary subsidy and dumping margins in November 1992 and January 1993, respectively. According to the American Institute for International Steel, the threat of penalty duties and the requirement that importers post bond or cash deposits to cover possible final imposition of duties, created shortages of some steel products. Immediately after the ruling, imports dropped sharply, by 45 percent from January to February, while import penetration fell from 18.8 to 11.4 percent in the same period (*Wall Street Journal*, 19 April 1993).

In its final determination of 22 June 1993, the Commerce Department concluded that dumping and subsidy margins ranged from 3.65 percent to 109.2 percent for the dumping cases and as high as 72.9 percent for the subsidy cases. On 27 July 1993, the US International Trade Commission ruled that US industry had been "materially injured" by steel imports in 32 of the 72 cases, affecting just over half ($1.733 billion) of the total imports originally subject to investigation ($3.441 billion).[1]

Methodological Notes

The US International Trade Commission reported to Congress in 1989 that the VRAs apparently had little impact on the US market in 1988,

---

1. On 30 September 1993, the petitioners announced that they had filed appeals with the Court of International Trade in the cases in which the USITC had found no injury. The petitioners also announced they would vigorously oppose any appeals brought by companies against whom duties were imposed.

primarily because of the sharp dollar depreciation between 1985 and 1987. Between 1988 and 1990, the market share of imported steel (other than semifinished) continued to fall, reaching 16.6 percent of apparent US consumption, well below the 19.1 percent ceiling set in the VRA program. Thus, we assume there was no protective impact of the VRAs in 1990, the base year for our estimates.

Here we have calculated the welfare effects of imposing the antidumping and countervailing duties (ADD and CVD) recently affirmed by the Department of Commerce and the US International Trade Commission. In performing these calculations, antidumping and countervailing duties are treated as any other tariff. No estimate is made of the improvement to global welfare that could result if the US imposition of penalty duties in fact serves to reduce distortions to world steel production and trade. For example, if US imposition of countervailing duties causes European governments to phase out their subsidy programs faster, this policy change would reduce global economic distortions. In particular, European countries would gain from putting investment resources to better use outside the steel industry.

The unfair trade petitions, filed by firms accounting for more than 80 percent of US production, targeted four categories of flat-rolled carbon steel, primarily produced by large integrated steel firms: plate, hot-rolled, cold-rolled, and corrosion-resistant flat steel products. Because these firms use some hot-rolled steel to make cold-rolled products, and cold-rolled to make corrosion-resistant products, data on open-market shipments (not including intra-company transfers) were used for domestic shipments in the model. Data on imports reflect shipments from all suppliers, whether or not targeted in the unfair trade cases, and also includes hot-rolled steel, even though the USITC found no injury for that category.

The estimated ad valorem equivalent of the ADD and CVD margins is a trade-weighted average of the final duty margins announced by the Department of Commerce on 22 June 1993 and affirmed by the USITC on 27 July. Since the ITA methodology purportedly adjusts dumping margins for any identified subsidy, the two types of duty are simply added when both apply to shipments of the same product from the same country. The own-price elasticities of demand for the domestic and imported products (E_{dd} and E_{mm}) are weighted averages of Robert Crandall's estimates for these products (Crandall 1981, 131).

Some observers predicted that a duty of 10 percent or more would be high enough to eliminate affected steel from the market altogether. Therefore, a second scenario (not shown) was estimated, reflecting the assumption that imported steel goods with ADD and CVD margins above 10 percent cease to be shipped. This scenario assumes no offsetting increases in supply from unrestricted suppliers; thus, as in other cases, the resulting calculations should be viewed as an upper-bound estimate of the possible effects of the ADDs and CVDs. This scenario predicts an import price effect of 19.5 percent, more than double that in the scenario summarized in the following table, and a consumer surplus loss of over $1.4 billion.

Effects of imposing CV and AD duties
(millions of dollars unless noted)

Consumer surplus loss	1,035
Producer surplus gain	657
Tariff revenue gain	318
Efficiency loss	59
Employment gain (number of workers)	1,239

Base-year data (1991)		Postrestriction estimates	
Import price (Pm) (dollars/short ton)	466	Import price (Pm') (dollars/short ton)	530
Import volume (Qm) (millions of short tons)	6.81	Import volume (Qm') (millions of short tons)	4.97
Domestic price (Pd) (dollars/short ton)	438	Domestic price (Pd') (dollars/short ton)	455
Domestic output (Qd) (millions of short tons)	37.58	Domestic output (Qd') (millions of short tons)	38.54
Employment (number of workers)	48,657	Employment (number of workers)	49,896

PARAMETERS

Elasticities		Constants		Price effects of barrier	
E_{dd}	−1.08	lna	7.00	Average ad valorem tariff[a] (percent)	5.2
E_{dm}	0.52	lnb	−0.33		
E_s	0.65	lnc	5.53		
E_{mm}	−3.25			Tariff equivalent of the ADDS and CVDs (percent)	13.8
E_{md}	2.69				
θ	0.3				

a. Unweighted average of the "normal" ad valorem duty rates for the affected categories (USITC Pub. No. 2549). The estimated welfare effects assume this normal tariff remains after elimination of the ADDs and CVDs.

Sources: USITC Pub. No. 2549 (1992, I-59, I-60, I-62, I-63, I-119, I-123); International Trade Administration (press release on final AD and CV duties); USITC (press release on final injury decision); Crandall (1981, 131, for E_{dd} and E_{mm}).

Semiconductors

In 1985 the US semiconductor industry and the US government accused the Japanese industry of engaging in unfair trading practices: selling semiconductors at "less than fair value" in the United States (i.e., dumping semiconductors) and restricting foreign access in the Japanese home market. In June 1985 the Semiconductor Industry Association (SIA) filed a petition with the US Trade Representative under Section 301 of the Trade Act of 1974 (as amended) complaining about the lack of market access in Japan. Shortly thereafter, Micron Technology filed a petition with the Department of Commerce alleging that Japanese producers were dumping 64K DRAM (dynamic random access memory) chips; in September, Intel, Advanced Micro Devices, and National Semiconductor followed with a petition alleging dumping of EPROM (erasable, programmable, read-only memory) chips; and, finally, in an unprecedented action, the Department of Commerce self-initiated a dumping investigation on DRAMs of 256K and above.[1]

In August 1986 the US and Japanese governments reached an agreement intended to resolve both the Section 301 and dumping investigations. In exchange for suspension of the Section 301 action, the Japanese indicated in a secret side letter that foreign market share in Japan should reach 20 percent by the end of the five-year agreement (up from about 10 percent). In exchange for suspension of the dumping investigations on EPROMs and 256K DRAMs and above, the Japanese firms agreed to provide information on their costs; the Department of Commerce then calculated "fair market values" (FMV) for each Japanese firm's sales.[2] Sales into the US market below the FMV price would be presumed to be dumped and would be subject to duties. The agreement thus established individual price floors for each Japanese firm, the assumption being that the firms would continue to compete on price, as long as each firm stayed above its own FMV. The agreement also provided for monitoring of Japanese sales to third countries to ensure that dumping in those markets did not make the United States a "high-price island" and thereby encourage US semiconductor users to move production offshore (Tyson 1992, 106–10).

---

1. 64K and 256K refer to the number of kilobytes (and 1M to a megabyte, consisting of a million bytes); these are measures of a chip's memory capacity.

2. The investigation on 64K DRAMs was concluded before the agreement was reached, and an average weighted duty of 20 percent was levied; for reasons explained below, however, the duties had little or no impact.

Effects of eliminating the Japanese cartel
(millions of dollars unless noted)

Consumer surplus gain	1,231
Producer surplus loss	257
Quota rent gain[a]	835
Efficiency gain	139
Employment loss (number of workers)	2,342

Base-year data (1989)		Postliberalization estimates	
Import price (Pm) (dollars/unit)	4.81	Import price (Pm') (dollars/unit)	3.85
Import volume (Qm) (millions of units)	870	Import volume (Qm') (millions of units)	1,159
Domestic price (Pd) (dollars/unit)	5.89	Domestic price (Pd') (dollars/unit)	5.40
Domestic output (Qd) (millions of units)	575	Domestic output (Qd') (millions of units)	484
Employment (production workers)	14,800	Employment (production workers)	12,458

PARAMETERS

Elasticities		Constants		Price effects of barrier	
E_{dd}	−1.80	lna	7.24	Average ad valorem tariff (percent)	0
E_{dm}	1.47	lnb	2.81		
E_s	2.00	lnc	7.56		
E_{mm}	−1.70			Tariff equivalent (percent)	25.0
E_{md}	1.06				
θ	.3				

a. In this case, the "quota rents" are the result of administrative guidance from the Japanese Ministry of International Trade and Industry limiting the output of Japanese chip manufacturers.

Sources: Census Bureau, *National Trade Databank; Current Industrial Reports;* Baldwin (1990, 18) for the elasticity of aggregate demand.

In early 1987 the United States retaliated against Japan for failing to halt dumping in third markets and for lack of progress on the commitment to increase US market share for chips in Japan. The retaliatory duties targeted $300 million in Japanese exports of products other than chips. The administration lifted the sanctions on $135 million of Japanese exports later in the year when it determined that the dumping in third markets had ceased. The $165 million in sanctions for continuing lack of market access continued until a new arrangement was negotiated in 1991.

Although the retaliatory sanctions obviously imposed costs on consumers of the affected products, the scenario examined in this case focuses on the effects of the part of the agreement that set floor prices to deal with dumping. In addressing the dumping, the Department of Commerce sought to minimize the costs to US purchasers of chips by preserving competition among Japanese firms; therefore, the department established individual FMVs for each firm rather than a common price floor. But the department's efforts were offset by Japanese measures. In order to enforce the dumping provisions of the agreement, MITI provided "administrative guidance" to firms producing in Japan regarding the level of output and exports, thus removing the incentive to compete on price. The agreement thus appears to have facilitated the formation of a MITI-led cartel among Japanese producers (Tyson 1992, 113–18). As Kenneth Flamm has noted,

> The irony of the 1986 agreement was that, after a decade of complaints by American producers over the role of MITI in issuing 'administrative guidance' to Japanese industry, U.S. trade policy helped create a regime that considerably reinforced MITI's power and influence over the Japanese semiconductor industry and encouraged Japanese producers to limit competition with each other (1991, 23).[3]

Methodological Notes

Because the semiconductor industry is rapidly evolving with the successive introduction of more powerful chips and rapid price declines, the results in this case, more so than in the others, must be viewed as restricted to a point in time. Because of technological change, for example, the antidumping duties imposed on 64K DRAMs in 1986 probably had little or no effect on prices in the United States because most users had already moved on to using the more technologically advanced 256K and later 1M chips (Baldwin 1990, 4–5).[4] Price effects for other chips

---

3. Flamm (1989, 7–18) provides a detailed discussion of MITI's actions in enforcing the semiconductor agreement.

4. The share in total US DRAM consumption of 64K DRAMs dropped from 69 percent in 1985 to less than 10 percent in 1989 (USITC Pub. No. 1862; *Current Industrial Reports*).

depend on where they are in the product cycle and the extent of market dominance of the Japanese producers.

Data reported in Tyson (115, 122) support the contention of Flamm (1989, 7–18) that MITI's "administrative guidance" was not fully effective until after the United States imposed sanctions in April 1987. Prices of 256K DRAMs and EPROMs, which had been steadily declining, stabilized in 1986 and the first half of 1987, then began rising in late 1987; prices of 1M DRAMs exhibited similar behavior. Tyson (1992, 123) argues that slumping demand and increased competition from South Korean producers began to destabilize the cartel in 1989 and that by 1990 the price effects of the suspension agreement were largely dissipated. Thus, in our analysis the behavior of the cartel is assumed to affect chip prices primarily from mid-1987 through the first half of 1989.

Prices for 256K EPROMs resumed their steady decline early in 1989, as did 1M DRAMs; 256K DRAM prices did not begin declining until mid-1989 and did not fall to preagreement levels until the first quarter of 1990. Because 256K DRAMs and EPROMs were further along in the product cycle than 1M DRAMs and because the downward trend in prices for these chips showed signs of stabilizing before the agreement was signed in August 1986, the average price of these chips during the eight quarters of cartel dominance (1987:3 through 1989:2) is compared with their average price during the two quarters immediately prior to that period (1987:1 and 1987:2) plus the two quarters after prices had returned to precartel levels.[5] For 1M DRAMs, which were at an earlier stage in the product cycle, prices declined steadily and rapidly until the last quarter of 1987; thus for these chips, the average price for the eight quarters from 1987:3 through 1989:2 is compared only with the average price for 1989:3 and 1989:4.

In EPROMs, US and European producers still controlled nearly 50 percent of the market, and the price impact was less severe than for DRAMs (Tyson 1992, 121–122; Flamm 1989, 18, fn. 40). Since prices of 1M EPROMs declined steadily throughout the period, the price effect on these chips is assumed to be zero. However, the price increase for 256K EPROMs is estimated as 25 percent. By contrast with the EPROM market, Japanese producers controlled between 70 and 80 percent of the global DRAM market in 1985–88 and over 90 percent of the 1M DRAM market (Tyson 1992, 108 and 120). The quarterly data on average selling prices (reported in Tyson 1992, 115) suggests that cartel behavior on the part of Japanese producers raised the prices of 256K and 1M DRAMs by about 40 percent above what they otherwise would have been.

---

5. For 256K EPROMs the "postcartel" quarters are 1989:3 and 1989:4; for 256K DRAMs, which stayed high in price longer, the postcartel quarters are 1990:1 and 1990:2.

The data used in our scenario are for all memory chips—all EPROMs and DRAMs, as well as electrically erasable programmable ROM (EEPROMs) and static RAM, (SRAMs). Hence, the tariff equivalent of approximately 25 percent used in the model represents a weighted average of the estimated price effects for each category of chip (including 0 percent for EEPROMs, for DRAMs smaller than 256K, and for EPROMs larger than 256K, which are included in the base-year data). Because of the way the data are collected, the weights for DRAMs include SRAMs, but the role of SRAMs was probably small.[6] A 25 percent tariff equivalent on average for memory chips is consistent with research cited by Flamm (1989, 16) that concluded price controls or output reductions might enable Japanese producers to maintain gross margins above costs of 20 to 25 percent.

Unfortunately, because of missing data for 1988, the weights used in calculating the average tariff equivalent and the base-year data used in calculating the welfare effects of the cartel's pricing behavior are for 1989 only.

The price elasticities of demand are estimated from an estimate by Finan and Amundsen (cited in Baldwin 1990, 18) that the aggregate elasticity of demand is -1.5. An elasticity of substitution of -2 is assumed.

---

6. Imports of SRAMs in 1991 were about a fifth of US imports of SRAMs and DRAMs together; however, if the distribution by size in the two categories is similar to that for US production, the share of SRAMs 256K and larger would be much smaller: SRAMs 80K and larger accounted for only about 3 percent of US combined output of SRAMs and DRAMs of that size in 1988. Moreover, Flamm (1989, 13) notes that there was some upward pressure on prices of SRAMs as producers shifted output from SRAMs to DRAMs to take advantage of the greater profitability of DRAMs.

Appendix III

Antidumping Summary

Antidumping Summary

Although the first US countervailing duty law was passed in 1892 and the first US antidumping statute was enacted in 1916, the extensive use of countervailing and antidumping orders to protect US industry is a comparatively recent phenomenon. Until the early 1970s, the US antidumping and countervailing duty statutes seldom resulted in the imposition of penalty duties. Of the 371 investigations under the antidumping statute between 1955 and 1968, only 12 resulted in the imposition of antidumping duties (ADDs), while 89 others were settled through agreement with foreign suppliers either to raise their prices or otherwise terminate "less than fair value" (LTFV) sales. Of the 200 plus investigations of alleged foreign government subsidies between 1934 and 1974, only 41 resulted in the imposition of countervailing duties (CVDs) in the United States (Destler 1992, 141).

ADDs are designed to stop foreign exporters from selling products in the US market at a price either below the price charged in their home markets or below their own costs of production. CVDs are designed to offset subsidies that foreign exporters receive from their governments.[1]

Between 1974 and 1988, Congress instituted several legislative changes that had a direct effect on dumping and subsidization decisions.[2] Changes to the ADD and CVD statutes in the Trade Act of 1974 and the implementing legislation for the Tokyo Round of multilateral trade negotiations in 1979 made it easier for petitioners to prove dumping or subsidization by their foreign competitors and to get relief. The Trade Act of 1974 enacted strict time limits on the procedures: the period allowed from initiation to final determination was set at 9 to 12 months for ADD cases (depending on the complexity of the case) and the period for CVD cases was set at 12 months. The act gave detailed specifications for the calculation of the relevant sales price to be used in determining the dumping margin. Further, the amendments allowed the administering agency to use average costs, rather than marginal costs, in calculating the dumping margin.[3]

While the 1979 Trade Agreements Act required that dumping or subsidization must result in "material injury" to domestic industry before an antidumping or countervailing duty can be imposed, and while the act increased the openness of US administrative procedures, it also included numerous other changes in the ADD and CVD laws that encouraged

---

1. For a technical and critical exposition of the US antidumping law, see Finger (1993).

2. The following draws heavily on Baldwin and Moore (1991).

3. In US antitrust law, pricing below marginal cost can raise suspicions of predatory behavior, but pricing below average cost is generally accepted as a permissible practice.

their use relative to other trade remedies, especially the "escape clause" (section 201 of the Trade Act of 1974). For example, the material-injury standard used in ADD and CVD cases is lower than the "serious injury" standard a party must meet to be eligible for relief in a section 201 escape clause case. The act also tightened the existing time limits and compressed the overall timetable, from initiation to final determination, to 235 days for ADD cases and 160 days for CVD cases.

Once a positive preliminary finding had been made, the act required the affected importer to post a deposit. By increasing uncertainty as to the ultimate price of imported merchandise, the required deposit can reduce imports before the investigations are completed.[4] The act broadened the grounds on which the Commerce Department could initiate ADD and CVD cases; for example, it explicitly lists a set of specific government actions that are considered to be actionable under the CVD statute. Finally, it transferred responsibility for determining dumping and subsidy margins from the Department of the Treasury to the Department of Commerce, in the belief that Commerce would enforce trade remedy measures more vigorously.

Proposed provisions on targeting subsidies, input dumping, and natural resources subsidization, which would have further broadened the scope of the ADD and CVD provisions, were not included in the final version of the Trade and Tariff Act of 1984. However, several other changes to the ADD and CVD statutes did tighten unfair trade remedies. First, a provision regarding "upstream" subsidies was enacted, although this merely codified Commerce's practice of including subsidized inputs that bestow a competitive benefit on the producer in its calculation of the CVD margin. The act established the Trade Remedy Assistance Office in the International Trade Commission to help small US businesses prepare petitions. Other changes in the law were designed to reduce the time and costs of obtaining confidential business information from respondents, to allow coalitions of petitioners to file a case, and to provide for the monitoring of suspect imports in order to encourage Commerce to initiate ADD and CVD cases.

The Omnibus Trade and Competitiveness Act of 1988 further tightened the unfair trade statutes by attacking methods devised by foreign firms for circumventing ADDs—in particular, the establishment of so-called "screwdriver plants" in the United States. The act provided that imported parts destined for assembly in the United States would be subject to ADDs or CVDs when the final product was subject to an ADD or CVD order. This provision was also extended to third-country

---

4. For example, according to the American Institute for International Steel, the threat of penalty duties caused by the recent round of ADD and CVD cases initiated by the US steel industry has already created a shortage of some steel products in the United States (*Inside US Trade*, 9 April 1993).

assembly and slightly altered imported goods. In addition, the act eliminated the drawback of ADD and CVD duties when the product was reexported and provided for the monitoring of downstream products made abroad from dumped or subsidized inputs. Finally, the act sought to discourage dumping practices by foreign producers in third countries, since those dumped goods could cause US exporters to lose in those markets.

This series of legislative changes, along with highly competitive conditions in global markets, resulted in an upsurge in "unfair" trade cases, as the antidumping and countervailing duty laws quickly became the instruments of choice for industries seeking trade relief. More cases were submitted under the ADD and CVD statutes, covering a far greater volume of imports, and more were decided in favor of the petitioning industries than had been the case.

Between 1980 and 1984, 249 countervailing duty and 221 antidumping investigations were initiated. From 1985 to 1989, the figures were 96 and 217 cases, respectively. Moreover, almost half of the countervailing duty and antidumping cases resulted either in an imposition of duties or suspension agreements under which foreign exporters agreed to raise prices or otherwise restrain sales in the US market. Many cases that were withdrawn before completion of the investigation were dropped because the source nation decided to instigate some form of export limitation (Destler 1992, 164).

Action under the countervailing duty statute saw its peak in the early 1980s. Of the 345 countervailing duty cases initiated between 1980 and 1990, 326 were launched through 1986, with 140 cases initiated in 1982 alone. These figures reflect the large number of petitions filed by the US steel industry against EC producers and a number of newly industrializing countries. After the voluntary export restraint (VER) regime for steel had been put in place over 1982–85, the number of newly initiated countervailing duty cases dropped significantly. From 1987 to 1990, just 33 cases were investigated. By contrast, the number of newly initiated antidumping cases remained high. The second half of the decade also showed a higher "success rate" for petitioners in antidumping, rising from 45 percent in the first half to 64 percent in the second half of the decade (table A.1).

While the number of ADD cases, the value of trade affected by those cases, and the average antidumping duty imposed on imports all appear to have increased sharply in the 1980s, the proportion of US imports affected by ADD orders in 1990 was only about 1 percent.[5] Table A.2 presents partial data on the 211 ADD orders in effect as of 1 January

---

5. This figure does not include informal industry-to-industry price undertakings because data on those agreements are not available. Inclusion of those cases, however, would not significantly change the proportion of US imports affected by antidumping measures.

Table A.1 Antidumping cases and results, 1980–89

Year	Total[a]	Petitions withdrawn	Investigations completed	Cases affirmed[b]		No dumping found		No injury found	
				Number	Percentage of cases completed	Number	Percentage of cases completed	Number	Percentage of cases completed
1980	21	9	12	3	25	1	8	8	67
1981	15	4	11	7	64	1	9	3	27
1982	65	24	41	14	34	3	7	24	59
1983	46	5	41	19	46	5	12	17	41
1984	74	42	32	12	38	5	16	15	47
1985	66	16	50	29	58	2	4	19	38
1986	71	7	64	44	69	3	5	17	27
1987	15	1	14	9	64	0	0	5	36
1988	42	0	42	22	52	3	7	17	40
1989	23	3	20	14	70	0	0	6	30
Total	438	111	327	173	53	23	7	131	40

a. Total number of petitions submitted during the year.
b. Cases resulting in an antidumping action.

Source: Reprinted from Destler (1992, 168).

1992. Of the 192 nonsteel-related cases, some 32 date from the 1960s and 1970s, while another 25 orders have been in place since the early 1980s.[6]

Data on trade values and duty levels are available for a subset of 119 nonsteel cases (62 percent of the total population of 192 such cases). More data are available for the more recent cases than for the older ones. Nevertheless, table A.2 suggests that the value of imports subject to ADD orders increased sharply in the mid-to-late 1980s. Excluding steel, the proportion of total imports in categories affected by ADD orders that were actually subject to duties increased to 68 percent since 1985, up from 50 percent for orders imposed earlier.

The average duty imposed in the nonsteel cases, weighted by affected imports, was 46 percent in 1991; when weighted by all imports in the affected categories, the average dropped to 31 percent. Although these duty levels are high relative to average US tariffs on dutiable manufactured goods of around 5 percent, they affect only a small fraction of the $480 billion of goods imported by the United States in 1991.

---

6. Cases involving steel are listed separately because of the prevalence of other trade policy interventions in this sector (see the case report on steel in appendix II). The steel cases included in table A.2 for the 1980s primarily reflect complaints brought against small suppliers not covered by VERs.

Table A.2 Outstanding US antidumping orders as of 1 January 1992

	Nonsteel product cases					Steel product cases (1960–91)[b]
	ADD Order imposed in[a]:					
	1960–79	1980–84	1985–88	1989–91	Total	
Total number of orders outstanding as of Jan. 1, 1992	32	25	71	64	192	19
Number of cases for which data are available[c]	3	8	54	54	119	12
Affected imports (millions of dollars)	6	88	1402	1716	3212	273
Total imports in affected categories (millions of dollars)	28	163	1939	2655	4785	3294
Affected imports as percentage of total imports	21.4	54.0	72.3	64.6	67.1	8.3

Average duty (percentages)

Simple	22.2	26.8	33.9	54.3	42.4	30.2
Weighted by affected imports	14.6	40.0	32.3	57.9	46.1	27.5
Weighted by total imports	3.0	21.6	23.4	37.4	31.0	2.3
Memo:						
Total US imports of goods	98,185	249,749	338,083	482,129		
(Year)	1975	1980	1985	1991		

a. The time periods correspond to changes in the antidumping law. The numbers in the columns refer to orders issued in that period and still ongoing as of the end of 1991. The numbers do not represent all orders issued in each period; they only show those still in place in 1991. These figures include formal suspension agreements, but there are another 12 cases with affirmative preliminary findings of "less than fair value" sales or injury in which the petitions were withdrawn before completion of the investigation. If there were informal, industry-to-industry price undertakings, they are not reflected here.

b. Steel product cases are listed separately since most steel products were affected by other trade restrictions (the trigger price mechanism in the late 1970s, "voluntary" export restraints in the early 1970s and most of the 1980s). These statistics reflect primarily cases brought against small suppliers not covered by the VERs.

c. Data on imports and calculated average duties are based on this subset of cases, the only ones for which data on both affected imports and total imports are available.

Appendix References

General

Unless otherwise indicated in the references for the specific case studies, domestic production, trade, and employment data are from the following official sources:

US Department of Commerce, Census Bureau
  Annual Survey of Manufacturers: Value of Product Shipments.
  Census of Manufacturers: Industry Series.
  Census of Manufacturers: Subject Series.
  Current Industrial Reports.
  EM-575. *U.S. Exports by 4-digit SIC-Based Product Code* (December).
  FT-447. *U.S. Exports, Harmonized Schedule B, Commodity by Country.*
  FT-990. *U.S. Merchandise Trade.*
  IM-146. *U.S. Imports for Consumption.*
  IM-175. *U.S. General Imports and Imports for Consumption* (December).
  National Trade Data Bank: U.S. Merchandise Export Trade—Commodity by Country.
  National Trade Data Bank: U.S. Merchandise Import Trade—Commodity by Country.
  Statistical Abstract of the United States: The National Data Book.
US Department of Commerce, International Trade Administration
  1985–93. *U.S. Industrial Outlook.*
US Department of Commerce, Office of Textiles and Apparel
  1992. *Major Shipper Report* (18 February).
US Department of Labor, Bureau of Labor Statistics
  1986–92. *Supplement to Employment and Earnings.*
  1986–92. *Supplement to Producer Prices and Price Indexes.*
US International Trade Commission
  1991. *U.S. Trade Shifts in Selected Commodity Areas—1990 Annual Report.* USITC Pub. 2380.
  1992. *U.S. Trade Shifts in Selected Commodity Areas—1991 Annual Report.* USITC Pub. 2517.

Summaries and Elasticities

Hufbauer, Gary Clyde, Diane E. Berliner, and Kimberly Ann Elliott. 1986. *Trade Protection in the United States: 31 Case Studies*. Washington: Institute for International Economics.

Tarr, David G. 1989. *A General Equilibrium Analysis of the Welfare and Employment Effects of US Quotas in Textiles, Autos and Steel*. Washington: Federal Trade Commission.

US International Trade Commission. 1989. *The Economic Effects of Significant U.S. Import Restraints, Phase I: Manufacturing*. USITC Pub. 2222. Washington: USITC.

US International Trade Commission. 1990a. *Estimated Tariff Equivalents of U.S. Quotas on Agricultural Imports and Analysis of Competitive Conditions in U.S. and Foreign Markets for Sugar, Meat, Peanuts, Cotton, and Dairy Products*. USITC Pub. 2276. Washington: USITC.

US International Trade Commission. 1990b. *The Economic Effects of Significant U.S. Import Restraints, Phase II: Agricultural Products and Natural Resources*. USITC Pub. 2314. Washington: USITC.

US International Trade Commission. 1990c. *The Economic Effects of Significant U.S. Import Restraints, Phase III: Services*. USITC Pub. 2422. Washington: USITC.

US International Trade Commission. 1991. *An Introduction to the ITC Computable General Equilibrium Model: Addendum to the Economic Effects of Significant U.S. Imports Restraints*. USITC Pub. 2423. Washington: USITC.

Appendix I: 21 Cases in Effect in 1990

Canned Tuna

US Department of Commerce, National Oceanic and Atmospheric Administration. 1991. *Fisheries of the United States, 1990*. Washington: NOAA.

US International Trade Commission. 1990. *Tuna: Competitive Conditions Affecting the U.S. and European Tuna Industries in Domestic and Foreign Markets*. USITC Pub. 2339. Washington: USITC.

Ceramic Tiles

Washington Economic Research Consultants. 1985. "Estimated Impact of Trade Remedies or Exchange Rate Revaluation on the US Ceramic Tile Industry." Prepared for Tile Council of America, Inc. Washington: Tile Council of America, Inc. (September).

Frozen Concentrated Orange Juice

Primo Braga, Carlos Alberto, and Silber, Simao Davi. 1991. *Brazilian Frozen Concentrated Orange Juice: The Folly of Unfair Trade Cases*. Washington: World Bank.

US Department of Agriculture, Foreign Agricultural Service. 1992. *Horticultural Products Review*. Washington: USDA (July and August).

US International Trade Commission. 1984. *Frozen Concentrated Orange Juice from Brazil*. USITC Pub. 1623. Washington: USITC.

Rubber Footwear

Footwear Industries of America. 1991. *Footwear Manual 1991*. Washington: Footwear Industries of America.

Softwood Lumber

US International Trade Commission. 1992. *Softwood Lumber from Canada*. USITC Pub. 2530. Washington: USITC.

US International Trade Commission. 1985. *Conditions Relating to the Importation of Softwood Lumber into the United States*. USITC Pub. 1765. Washington: USITC.

Richardson, David R. and John H. Mutti. 1976. "Industrial Displacement through Environment Controls: The International Competitive Aspect." In Ingo Walter, *Studies in International Environmental Economics.* New York: John Wiley & Sons.

Women's Footwear

Footwear Industries of America. 1991. *Footwear Manual 1991.* Washington: Footwear Industries of America.

Dairy

Federal Trade Commission, Bureau of Economics. 1990. *Effects of U.S. Import Restraints on Agricultural and Other Products: General Equilibrium Results.* Washington: Federal Trade Commission.

Flynn, Joseph E., and Kenneth A. Reinert. 1992. *The Welfare and Resource Allocation Implications of the U.S. Dairy Quotas.* Office of Economics, Research Division Working Paper No. 92-02-A. Washington: US International Trade Commission.

Hornig, E., R. Boisvert, and D. Blandford. 1990. "Explaining the Distribution of Quota Rents from U.S. Cheese Imports." *Australian Journal of Agricultural Economics:* 421–34.

US International Trade Commission. Office of Industries. 1992. *Industry & Trade Summary: Dairy Produce.* USITC Pub. 2477. Washington: USITC.

Peanuts

US International Trade Commission. 1990. *Estimated Tariff Equivalents of U.S. Quotas on Agricultural Imports and Analysis of Competitive Conditions in U.S. and Foreign Markets for Sugar, Meat, Peanuts, Cotton, and Dairy Products.* USITC Pub. 2276. Washington: USITC.

US International Trade Commission. 1991. *Peanuts.* USITC Pub. 2369. Washington: USITC.

Sugar

Australian Bureau of Agricultural and Resource Economics. 1990. *1990 and US Sugar Policy Reform.* Canberra: Australian Government Publishing Service.

Barry, Robert D. 1991. "The U.S. and World Sugar Markets: Government Policies, Market Distortions, and Prospects for Change." Paper presented to the Wisconsin Rural Leadership, Washington, D.C. (11 March).

Federal Trade Commission, Bureau of Economics. 1990. *Effects of U.S. Import Restraints on Agricultural and Other Products: General Equilibrium Results.* Washington: FTC.

Maskus, Keith E. 1989. "Large Costs and Small Benefits of the American Sugar Programme." *The World Economy* (Spring): 85–104.

Tarr, David G., and Morris E. Morkre. 1984. *Aggregate Costs to the United States of Tariffs and Quotas on Imports: General Tariff Cuts and Removal of Quotas on Automobiles, Steel, Sugar, and Textiles.* Washington: Bureau of Economics, Federal Trade Commission.

Tyers, Rod, and Kym Anderson. 1989. "Price Elasticities in International Food Trade: Synthetic Estimates from a Global Model." *Journal of Policy Modeling,* 11, no. 3: 315–44.

US Department of Agriculture, Economic Research Service. 1990. *Sugar: Background for 1990 Farm Legislation.* Washington: USDA.

US Department of Agriculture, Economic Research Service. 1991. *Sugar and Sweetener: Situation and Outlook Yearbook.* Washington: USDA.

Maritime

Eno Transportation Foundation. 1992. *Transportation in America.* Washington: Eno Transportation Foundation.

US Army Corps of Engineers. 1990. *Waterborne Commerce of the United States, 1989.* Washington: Government Printing Office.

US International Trade Commission. 1992a. *Commercial Policy and the Domestic Carrying Trade: A General Equilibrium Assessment.* Washington: USITC.

US International Trade Commission. 1992b. *Shipbuilding Trade Reform Act of 1992: Likely Economic Effects of Enactment.* USITC Pub. No. 2495. Washington: USITC.

Textiles and Apparel

Cline, William R. 1990. *The Future of World Trade in Textiles and Apparel.* Washington: Institute for International Economics.

Erzan, R., K. Krishna, and L. H. Tan. 1991. *Rent Sharing in the Multi-Fibre Arrangement: Theory and Evidence from US Apparel Imports from Hong Kong.* Policy, Research and External Affairs Working Paper 597. Washington: World Bank.

General Agreement on Tariffs and Trade. 1986. *Extension of the Multifibre Agreement Agreed.* Geneva: GATT.

Goto, J. 1989. "The Multifibre Arrangement and its Effects on Developing Countries." *World Bank Research Observer* 4: 203–27.

Reinert, Kenneth A. 1993. "Textile and Apparel Protection in the United States: A General Equilibrium Analysis." *The World Economy* 16, no. 3 (May): 359–76.

Machine Tools

Hooley, Richard. 1987. *Protection for the Machine Tool Industry: Domestic and International Negotiations for Voluntary Restraint Agreements.* Pew Case No. 13. Pittsburg: University of Pittsburgh.

National Machine Tool Builders Association. 1990. *Annual Industry Handbook.* McLean, VA: NMTBA.

Reinert, Kenneth A., and David W. Roland-Holst. 1992. "Disaggregated Armington Elasticities for the Mining and Manufacturing Sectors of the United States." *Journal of Policy Modeling* 14, no. 5.

US General Accounting Office, National Security and International Affairs Division. 1990. *Revitalizing the Machine Tool Industry.* Washington: Government Printing Office (July).

Appendix II: Cases Not Effective in 1990

Automobiles

Dinopoulos, Elias, and Mordechai E. Kreinen. 1988. "Effects of the U.S.-Japan Auto VER on European Prices and on U.S. Welfare." *The Review of Economics and Statistics* 70, no. 3.

Feenstra, Robert C. 1984. "Voluntary Export Restraint in U.S. Autos 1980–81: Quality, Employment, and Welfare Effects." In Robert Baldwin and Anne O. Krueger, *The Structure and Evolution of Recent U.S. Trade Policy.* Chicago: University of Chicago Press for the National Bureau of Economic Research.

Jones, Kent. 1989. *Exporter Adjustment to Voluntary Export Restraint: The Case of Quality Upgrading by Japanese Auto Manufacturers.* PAS WP/89/15. Washington: Department of State.

de Melo, Jaime, and David G. Tarr. 1990. "Welfare Costs of U.S. Quotas in Textiles, Steel and Autos." *The Review of Economics and Statistics* 72, no. 3 (August).

Tarr, David. 1989. *A General Equilibrium Analysis of the Welfare and Employment Effects of US Quotas in Textiles, Autos and Steel.* Washington: Federal Trade Commission.

US International Trade Commission. 1985. *A Review of Recent Developments in the U.S. Automobiles Industry Including an Assessment of the Japanese Voluntary Restraint Agreements.* USITC Pub. 1648. Washington: USITC.

US International Trade Commission. 1992. *Minivans from Japan.* Pub. No. 2529. Washington: USITC.

Wards Automotive Yearbook. 1991. Detroit: Ward's Communications.

Flat-Rolled Steel Products

Crandall, Robert W. 1981. *The U.S. Steel Industry in Recurrent Crisis: Policy Options in a Competitive World*. Washington: The Brookings Institution.

US Department of Commerce, International Trade Administration. 1993. *Final Determinations: Commerce Finds 19 Countries Dump Carbon Steel Products; 12 Also Subsidize*. ITA 93-49. Washington: ITA.

US International Trade Commission. 1990. *Monthly Report on the Status of the Steel Industry*. USITC Pub. 2248. Washington: USITC.

US International Trade Commission. 1992. *Certain Flat Rolled Carbon Steel Products From Argentina, Australia, Austria, Belgium, Brazil, Canada, Finland, France, Germany, Italy, Japan, Korea, Mexico, The Netherlands, New Zealand, Poland, Romania, Spain, Sweden, Taiwan, and the United Kingdom*. USITC Pub. 2549. Washington: USITC.

Semiconductors

Baldwin, Richard. 1990. *The US-Japan Semiconductor Agreement*. Discussion Paper 387. London: Centre for Economic Policy Research.

Flamm, Kenneth. 1989. "Policy and Politics in the International Semiconductor Industry." Paper presented to the SEMI ISS Seminar. Newport Beach, California (16 January).

Flamm, Kenneth. 1991. "Making New Rules: High-Tech Trade Friction and the Semiconductor Industry." *The Brookings Review* (Spring): 22–29.

Tyson, Laura D'Andrea. 1992. *Who's Bashing Whom? Trade Conflict in High-Technology Industries*. Washington: Institute for International Economics.

US International Trade Commission. 1986. *64K Dynamic Random Access Memory Components From Japan*. USITC Pub. 1862. Washington: USITC.

Appendix III: Antidumping Summary

Baldwin, Robert E., and Michael O. Moore. 1991. "The Political Aspects of the Administration of the Trade Remedy Laws." In Richard Boltuck and Robert E. Litan, *Down in the Dumps: Administration of the Unfair Trade Laws*. Washington: The Brookings Institution.

Boltuck, Richard, and Robert E. Litan, eds. 1991. *Down in the Dumps: Administration of the Unfair Trade Laws*. Washington: The Brookings Institution.

Destler, I. M. 1992. *American Trade Politics*. Washington: Institute for International Economics.

Finger, J. Michael, ed. 1993. *Antidumping: How It Works and Who Gets Hurt*. Ann Arbor: The University of Michigan Press.

Other Publications from the
Institute for International Economics

POLICY ANALYSES IN INTERNATIONAL ECONOMICS Series

1 The Lending Policies of the International Monetary Fund
   John Williamson/*August 1982*
             ISBN paper 0-88132-000-5   72 pp.

2 "Reciprocity": A New Approach to World Trade Policy?
   William R. Cline/*September 1982*
             ISBN paper 0-88132-001-3   41 pp.

3 Trade Policy in the 1980s
   C. Fred Bergsten and William R. Cline/*November 1982*
   (out of print)   ISBN paper 0-88132-002-1   84 pp.
   Partially reproduced in the book *Trade Policy in the 1980s.*

4 International Debt and the Stability of the World Economy
   William R. Cline/*September 1983*
             ISBN paper 0-88132-010-2   134 pp.

5 The Exchange Rate System, Second Edition
   John Williamson/*September 1983, rev. June 1985*
   (out of print)   ISBN paper 0-88132-034-X   61 pp.

6 Economic Sanctions in Support of Foreign Policy Goals
   Gary Clyde Hufbauer and Jeffrey J. Schott/*October 1983*
             ISBN paper 0-88132-014-5   109 pp.

7 A New SDR Allocation?
   John Williamson/*March 1984*
             ISBN paper 0-88132-028-5   61 pp.

8 An International Standard for Monetary Stabilization
   Ronald I. McKinnon/*March 1984*
             ISBN paper 0-88132-018-8   108 pp.

9 The Yen/Dollar Agreement: Liberalizing Japanese Capital Markets
   Jeffrey A. Frankel/*December 1984*
             ISBN paper 0-88132-035-8   86 pp.

10 Bank Lending to Developing Countries: The Policy Alternatives
   C. Fred Bergsten, William R. Cline, and John Williamson/*April 1985*
             ISBN paper 0-88132-032-3   221 pp.

11 Trading for Growth: The Next Round of Trade Negotiations
   Gary Clyde Hufbauer and Jeffrey J. Schott/*September 1985*
             ISBN paper 0-88132-033-1   109 pp.

12 Financial Intermediation Beyond the Debt Crisis
   Donald R. Lessard and John Williamson/*September 1985*
             ISBN paper 0-88132-021-8   130 pp.

13 The United States-Japan Economic Problem
   C. Fred Bergsten and William R. Cline/*October 1985, 2d ed. January 1987*
             ISBN paper 0-88132-060-9   180 pp.

BOOKS

International Debt: Systemic Risk and Policy Response
William R. Cline/1984
                    ISBN cloth 0-88132-015-3   336 pp.

Trade Protection in the United States: 31 Case Studies
Gary Clyde Hufbauer, Diane E. Berliner, and Kimberly Ann Elliott/1986
                    ISBN paper 0-88132-040-4   371 pp.

Toward Renewed Economic Growth in Latin America
Bela Balassa, Gerardo M. Bueno, Pedro-Pablo Kuczynski, and Mario Henrique
Simonsen/1986
(out of stock)   ISBN paper 0-88132-045-5   205 pp.

Capital Flight and Third World Debt
Donald R. Lessard and John Williamson, editors/1987
(out of print)   ISBN paper 0-88132-053-6   270 pp.

The Canada-United States Free Trade Agreement:
The Global Impact
Jeffrey J. Schott and Murray G. Smith, editors/1988
                    ISBN paper 0-88132-073-0   211 pp.

World Agricultural Trade: Building a Consensus
William M. Miner and Dale E. Hathaway, editors/1988
                    ISBN paper 0-88132-071-3   226 pp.

Japan in the World Economy
Bela Balassa and Marcus Noland/1988
                    ISBN paper 0-88132-041-2   306 pp.

America in the World Economy: A Strategy for the 1990s
C. Fred Bergsten/1988
                    ISBN cloth 0-88132-089-7   235 pp.
                    ISBN paper 0-88132-082-X   235 pp.

Managing the Dollar: From the Plaza to the Louvre
Yoichi Funabashi/1988, 2d ed. 1989
                    ISBN paper 0-88132-097-8   307 pp.

United States External Adjustment and the World Economy
William R. Cline/May 1989
                    ISBN paper 0-88132-048-X   392 pp.

Free Trade Areas and U.S. Trade Policy
Jeffrey J. Schott, editor/May 1989
                    ISBN paper 0-88132-094-3   400 pp.

Dollar Politics: Exchange Rate Policymaking in the United States
I. M. Destler and C. Randall Henning/September 1989
                    ISBN paper 0-88132-079-X   192 pp.

Latin American Adjustment: How Much Has Happened?
John Williamson, editor/April 1990
                    ISBN paper 0-88132-125-7   480 pp.

The Future of World Trade in Textiles and Apparel
William R. Cline/1987, 2d ed. June 1990
                    ISBN paper 0-88132-110-9   344 pp.

Completing the Uruguay Round: A Results-Oriented Approach to the GATT Trade Negotiations
Jeffrey J. Schott, editor/*September 1990*
ISBN paper 0-88132-130-3   256 pp.

Economic Sanctions Reconsidered (in two volumes)
  Economic Sanctions Reconsidered: History and Current Policy
  (also sold separately, see below)
  Economic Sanctions Reconsidered: Supplemental Case Histories
  Gary Clyde Hufbauer, Jeffrey J. Schott, and Kimberly Ann Elliott/*1985, 2d ed.*
    December 1990
ISBN cloth 0-88132-115-X   928 pp.
ISBN paper 0-88132-105-2   928 pp.

Economic Sanctions Reconsidered: History and Current Policy
Gary Clyde Hufbauer, Jeffrey J. Schott, and Kimberly Ann Elliott/*December 1990*
ISBN cloth 0-88132-136-2   288 pp.
ISBN paper 0-88132-140-0   288 pp.

Pacific Basin Developing Countries: Prospects for the Future
Marcus Noland/*January 1991*
ISBN cloth 0-88132-141-9   250 pp.
ISBN paper 0-88132-081-1   250 pp.

Currency Convertibility in Eastern Europe
John Williamson, editor/*October 1991*
ISBN cloth 0-88132-144-3   396 pp.
ISBN paper 0-88132-128-1   396 pp.

Foreign Direct Investment in the United States
Edward M. Graham and Paul R. Krugman/*1989, 2d ed. October 1991*
ISBN paper 0-88132-139-7   200 pp.

International Adjustment and Financing: The Lessons of 1985-1991
C. Fred Bergsten, editor/*January 1992*
ISBN paper 0-88132-112-5   336 pp.

North American Free Trade: Issues and Recommendations
Gary Clyde Hufbauer and Jeffrey J. Schott/*April 1992*
ISBN cloth 0-88132-145-1   392 pp.
ISBN paper 0-88132-120-6   392 pp.

American Trade Politics
I. M. Destler/*1986, rev. June 1992*
ISBN cloth 0-88132-164-8   400 pp.
ISBN paper 0-88132-188-5   400 pp.

Narrowing the U.S. Current Account Deficit
Allen J. Lenz/*June 1992*
ISBN cloth 0-88132-148-6   640 pp.
ISBN paper 0-88132-103-6   640 pp.

The Economics of Global Warming
William R. Cline/*June 1992*
ISBN cloth 0-88132-150-8   416 pp.
ISBN paper 0-88132-132-X   416 pp.

U.S. Taxation of International Income: Blueprint for Reform
Gary Clyde Hufbauer, assisted by Joanna M. van Rooij/*October 1992*
	ISBN cloth 0-88132-178-8	304 pp.
	ISBN paper 0-88132-134-6	304 pp.

Who's Bashing Whom? Trade Conflict in High-Technology Industries
Laura D'Andrea Tyson/*November 1992*
	ISBN cloth 0-88132-151-6	352 pp.
	ISBN paper 0-88132-106-0	352 pp.

Korea in the World Economy
Il Sakong/*January 1993*
	ISBN cloth 0-88132-184-2	328 pp.
	ISBN paper 0-88132-106-0	328 pp.

NAFTA: An Assessment
Gary Clyde Hufbauer and Jeffrey J. Schott/*February 1993, rev. ed. October 1993*
	ISBN paper 0-88132-199-0	216 pp.

Pacific Dynamism and the International Economic System
C. Fred Bergsten and Marcus Noland, editors/*May 1993*
	ISBN paper 0-88132-196-6	424 pp.

Economic Consequences of Soviet Disintegration
John Williamson, editor/*May 1993*
	ISBN paper 0-88132-190-7	664 pp.

Reconcilable Differences? United States–Japan Economic Conflict
C. Fred Bergsten and Marcus Noland/*June 1993*
	ISBN paper 0-88132-129-X	296 pp.

Does Foreign Exchange Intervention Work?
Kathryn M. Dominguez and Jeffrey A. Frankel/*September 1993*
	ISBN 0-88132-104-4	192 pp.

Sizing Up U.S. Export Disincentives
J. David Richardson/*September 1993*
	ISBN 0-88132-107-9	192 pp.

Adjusting to Volatile Energy Prices
Philip K. Verleger, Jr./*November 1993*
	ISBN 0-88132-069-2	288 pp.

The Political Economy of Policy Reform
John Williamson, editor/*January 1994*
	ISBN 0-88132-195-8	624 pp.

Measuring the Costs of Protection in the United States
Gary Clyde Hufbauer and Kimberly Ann Elliott/*January 1994*
	ISBN 0-88132-108-7	144 pp.

SPECIAL REPORTS

1 **Promoting World Recovery: A Statement on Global Economic Strategy by Twenty-six Economists from Fourteen Countries/**
December 1982
(out of print)	ISBN paper 0-88132-013-7	45 pp.

FORTHCOMING

Greening the GATT
Daniel Esty

Foreign Direct Investment, Third Edition
Edward M. Graham and Paul R. Krugman

Global Competition Policy
Edward M. Graham and J. David Richardson

International Monetary Policymaking in the United States, Germany, and Japan
C. Randall Henning

The New Europe in the World Economy
Gary Clyde Hufbauer

Prospects for Western Hemisphere Economic Integration
Gary Clyde Hufbauer and Jeffrey J. Schott

China in the World Economy
Nicolas Lardy

Measuring the Costs of Protection in Japan
Yoko Sazanami, Shujiro Urata, and Hiroki Kawai

The Uruguay Round: An Assessment
Jeffrey J. Schott

The Future of the World Trading System
John Whalley

Trading and the Environment: Setting the Rules
John Whalley and Peter Uimonen

Equilibrium Exchange Rates: An Update
John Williamson

For orders outside the US and Canada please contact:

Longman Group UK Ltd.
PO Box 88
Harlow, Essex CM 19 5SR
UK

Telephone Orders: 0279 623925
Fax: 0279 453450
Telex: 817484